THE ART OF HUNTING

By Norman Strung

NORM STRUNG has authored 14 books and more than 1000 magazine articles on outdoor topics. He formerly operated a hunting and fishing guide service out of his log home near Bozeman, Montana. He has been a full-time freelance writer since 1968.

LARRY R. NELSON, a professional wildlife biologist, is also an experienced hunter. He has pursued everything from woodcock and wild turkey in his home state of Minnesota to elk and mule deer in the Rocky Mountains.

COWLES
Creative Publishing

A Division of Cowles Enthusiast Media, Inc.

President/COO: Nino Tarantino
Executive V. P./Editor-in-Chief: William B. Jones
THE ART OF HUNTING
Author: Norman Strung
Technical Advisor: Larry R. Nelson
Project Director: Dick Sternberg
Editorial Director: Chuck Wechsler
Production Director: Christine Watkins
Art Directors: Cy DeCosse, Delores Swanson
Director of Photography: Buck Holzemer
Staff Photographers: Bill Lindner, Jerry Robb
Project Manager: Teresa Marrone
Chief Researchers: Joseph Cella, Jay Strangis
Studio Manager: Elizabeth Woods
Production Staff: Michelle Alexander, Jim Bindas, Julie Churchill, Lowell Holland, Christopher Lentz, Tim Minkkinen, Nancy Nardone, Tom Nordby, Jean Sherlock, Jennie Smith, Nik Wogstad
Contributing Photographers: Grady Allen; Erwin & Peggy Bauer; Les & Craig Blacklock; David Books; Tom Brakefield; Hanson Carroll; Art Carter; Jon E. Cates; Glenn D. Chambers; Charlton Photos; Tim Christie; Herbert Clarke; Daniel J. Cox; Cy DeCosse; Charles H. Dickey; Ed Dutch; John Ebeling; Federal Cartridge Corporation; Al Gardner; Greg Gersbach; Gordon Gullion; Darrell Ivy; Larry D. Jones; Leonard Kamsler, by permission of Sports Afield, Inc.; Mark LaBarbera; Tom Mangelsen; Tom Martinson; Jay Massey; Margaret Thompson Mathewson; Worth Mathewson; Paul and Pete McLain; Bill McRae; Wyman Meinzer; Anthony Mercieca; Minnesota Department of Natural Resources; Gary Moss;

William H. Mullins; Doug Murphy; Nebraska Game and Parks Commission; LuRay Parker, Wyoming Game and Fish Department; Bill Reeves; Jerome B. Robinson; Lynn Rogers; Leonard Lee Rue III; Dwight Schuh; Ron Shade; Jerry Smith; Richard P. Smith; Dale Spartas; Ron Spomer; Dick Sternberg; Jay Strangis; Norm Strung; Sil Strung; Phil and Judy Sublett; Delores Swanson; Mitchell Thompson; Russ Tinsley; Frank Todd; Tom Ulrich; U.S.D.A. Forest Service; Charles F. Waterman; Chuck Wechsler; Ron Winch; James Zacks; Gary Zahm

Special Consultant: Bill Stevens, Federal Cartridge Corporation
Consultants: John Beech; John Beecham, Idaho Department of Fish and Game; Al Berner, Nick Gulden, Jack Heather, Tom Isley, Pat Karns, Dick Kimmel, Bill Longley, Minnesota Department of Natural Resources; Don Christisen, John Lewis, Ken Sadler, Missouri Department of Conservation; Cader Cox, Riverview Plantation; Ron George, Charles Winkler, Texas Parks & Wildlife Department; Bob Gilsvik; Alan, Bob and Brian Guffey, Hi Point Kennels & Hunting Club; Gordon Gullion, Forest Wildlife Project; Rick Hacker; Ed Harris, National Rifleman; Neil Hinton, Gail Martin, Martin Archery, Inc.; Dick Idol; Ron Ives, Mike Larsen, Federal Cartridge Corporation; Carl Johnson; Larry D. Jones; Charlie Kroll, Bear Archery; Bill Marshall; Gerald Moore, South Carolina Wildlife & Marine Resources; Ray Norrgard, Minnesota Waterfowl Association; Rich Olson, Wyoming Game and Fish Department; Larry Phairis, Fred Ward, Arkansas Game and Fish; Richard Phillips, University of Minnesota; Dale & Arlene Pitts, The Archery Hut; Lynn Rogers, North Central Forest Experiment Station; John Schneider; Jack Scovil; Larry Shoutz; Gene Smith, National Wild Turkey Federation; Phil Smith, Arizona Game and Fish Department; Ken Solomon, South Dakota Game, Fish and Parks Department; Russ Tinsley; Harrison B. Tordoff, Bell Museum of Natural History; J. Bruce Warren; Elroy Wildhaber; Gary Will, Idaho Fish and Game Department
Cooperating Agencies and Individuals: Anthony L. Aeschliman, The Marlin Firearms Co.; Baker Manufacturing Co.; Barr Taxidermy; Melvin J. Baughman, Dwight Burkhardt, Pat Redig, University of Minesota; Bear Archery; Beretta U.S.A. Corp.; Bill Berg, Bob Jessen, Bob Johnson, Minnesota Department of Natural Resources; Robert W. Blackstock, Wild Wings of Oklahoma; Herman Bockstruck, Glen Boeker, John Falk, Mike Jordan, Winchester Group, Olin Corporation; Buck Knives, Inc.; Burger Brothers Sporting Goods; Bushnell Optical Co.–Bausch & Lomb; Carry-Lite Decoys; W.R. Case & Sons Cutlery Co.; Chicago Cutlery; Coleman Co., Inc.; John Crawford, Oregon State University; Decoys Unlimited; Ralph Denney, Oregon Department of Fish and Wildlife; Dick Dietz, Ken Green, Remington Arms Company, Inc.; Dixie Gun Works, Inc.; Dr. Andrew Edin; Glenn Erickson, Montana Department of Fish, Wildlife and Parks; Bill Erpelding; Dave Fackler, Ballistic Products, Inc.; Ron Fowler, South Dakota Game, Fish and Parks Department; Elvon and Roger Fritz; Logan Grant, Metro Archery Center; Graphlex–Gordon Plastics, Inc.; Steve Grooms; Harry Harju, Wyoming Game and Fish Department; Harrington & Richardson, Inc.; Evan Hazard, Bemidji State University; Willard Henson; Bob Hernbrode, Colorado Division of Wildlife; Ithaca Gun Co.; Larry Jennings, Alaska Department of Fish and Game; Charles Jonkel, University of Montana; Rob Keck, James Earl Kennamer, National Wild Turkey Federation; John Kellner; Mark LaBarbera; Michael Lapinski; Gary Larson, South Dakota State University; David Loftis; Lohman Mfg. Co., Inc.; Lund American, Inc.; Lyman Products Corporation; Mallardtone Game Calls; Larry Marchinton, University of Georgia; Gordon McClain, Redfield; Dale McCullough, University of California; Henry Murkin, Delta Waterfowl Research Center; Dietland Muller-Schwarze, State University of New York; Tink Nathan, Safariland; National Rifle Association of America; National Shooting Sports Foundation, Inc.; Gary V. Nelson; Harold Nesbitt, Boone and Crockett Club; LaWaina and Ken Oelkers; P.S. Olt Co.; Outdoorsman, Intl.; Nick Painovich, Zippel Bay Resort; Randy Pannel, Hillbilly Squirrel Hunters Association; Don Parsons, Ammo Craft; Penquin Industries, Inc.; Penn's Woods Products, Inc.; Quack Decoy Corp.; Quaker Boy Turkey Calls; Rob Rainwater, Fred Parnell's The Sports Shop; Charles Ramsey, Texas A&M University; Savage Arms; Tom Schweitzer, Tom's Archery Shop; Jeff Shaer; James and Ida Shaffer, Shaffer and Associates, Inc.; Bill Siems, Federal Cartridge Corporation; Jack Slosson, California Department of Fish and Game; Bill Smith, Arizona Game and Fish Department; Smith & Wesson Co.; Sports Innovations, Inc.; San Stiver, Nevada Department of Wildlife; Sturm, Ruger & Company, Inc.; Super Yelper Turkey Calls; Daniel Sutcliffe, New Mexico Department of Game and Fish; Bob and Karen Swanson, Marsh Lake Hunting Preserve, Inc.; Swift Instruments, Inc.; Thompson/Center Arms; Gildo Tori, Ohio Department of Natural Resources; Robert Towry, Colorado Division of Wildlife; Utica Duxbak Corporation; Joel Vance, Missouri Department of Conservation; Tom Walters, The Ontario Federation of Anglers and Hunters; Clay Ward; John Ward, Wild Wings of Oneka; Dwain Warner, Bell Museum of Natural History; Washington Department of Game; W. R. Weaver Company; Robert E. Weet, Scotch Game Call Company Inc.; Jim Westberg, Muzzleloaders Etcetera, Inc.; Wilderness Sound Productions; Gary R. Williams, Leupold & Stevens, Inc.; Jim Wooly, Iowa Conservation Commission; Yentzen Sure Shot; James Zacks, Michigan State University; Dave Ziegler, Browning
Printing: R. R. Donnelley & Sons Co.

99 98 97 96 / 5 4 3 2 1

COWLES
Enthusiast Media

President/COO: Philip L. Penny

Contents

Introduction

Whether you pursue mule deer in the Rockies or cottontails in a thicket near your home, the sport of hunting offers a unique challenge. You must out-smart a wild animal that has a better knowledge of its environment and more highly-developed senses than your own.

This challenge, along with the camaraderie that goes hand in hand with hunting, accounts for the sport's tremendous popularity. And a successful hunter can enjoy a supply of lean, nutritious, un-tainted meat.

The Art of Hunting is intended to make you a better hunter. Each section of the book deals with a differ-ent facet of the sport. Together, they will help you develop the skills and savvy needed to consistently bag wild game.

The first section, *All About Wild Game,* will im-prove your understanding of wildlife behavior and help you to recognize good habitat. By knowing how animals sense danger, react to threats, and find food, water and cover, you can improve your chances of being in the right spot at the right time.

Skills and Equipment gives you all the information you need to select rifles, shotguns, bows and arrows, and even muzzleloaders. You will also learn how to choose the best ammunition for the game you hunt and how to become a proficient shooter. A re-markable series of through-the-scope photographs helps you choose the best sighting device for your type of hunting. This section goes far beyond the basics, explaining complex principles of bullet and shot performance with descriptive photos and easy-to-understand charts.

Hunting Strategies gets you started right by showing you how to plan your hunt and how to scout a potential spot to make sure it holds game. This section details the most popular hunting techniques,

from stalking to driving. You will learn how to tailor your hunting strategy to the terrain and time of day. The section also provides valuable tips for recover-ing downed game.

The final section, *Hunting Wild Game,* acquaints you with the continent's most popular game ani-mals. Hundreds of informative how-to-photos, along with a fact-filled text, help you locate, pursue and bag each of these species.

Astounding photography puts you in the hunting scene. You will experience the spine-tingling thrill of facing-off with a huge bull moose at 30 feet; the pulse-stopping excitement of a ring-necked pheas-ant bursting from cover at your feet; and the nerve-wracking anticipation of waiting for a wild turkey to strut close enough for a shot.

The hunting techniques shown in this book are those considered most effective by the nation's top hunting authorities. Hunting regulations and legal equipment differ in every state and province, so it is possible that some of the procedures described are illegal in your area. Baiting bears, for instance, is a popular method in some states, but is against the law in many others. Check the hunting laws if there is any question on a technique's legality.

In addition to the proven high-percentage hunting methods, this book will also reveal dozens of little known but effective tips that help the experts bag their game. You will learn how to attract diving ducks by waving a black flag and how to imitate a scolding squirrel by clicking quarters.

This book is a unique blend of straightforward writ-ing and captivating photography. Never before has so much how-to hunting information and so many dramatic wildlife photographs been packed into one volume. *The Art of Hunting* is sure to make your days afield more enjoyable — and more successful.

All About Wild Game

Understanding Game Populations

From the moment its life begins, a game animal faces threats from predators, weather, disease, and competition from its own kind. Only the strongest and wariest offspring live to reproduce. In this way, nature continually selects the best breeding stock to insure that the species will survive.

All game animals have the potential to produce many more young than the habitat can support. Reproductive rates are especially high among small game and upland birds. High mortality rates are nature's way of keeping game populations in check. When too many animals survive, a population explosion results, causing disease, stunted growth, and eventually starvation.

Among most upland birds, waterfowl and small game, 60 to 80 percent of the population dies each year. Individuals over 1 year old comprise only 20 to 40 percent of the fall population. Because young animals are more abundant and because they lack the savvy of older individuals, they make up the bulk of the hunter's bag.

Big game populations have a relatively low reproductive potential. The average animal lives longer and fall populations contain a higher percentage of older individuals, usually from 65 to 85 percent.

Hunting regulations are based on the concept that game can be harvested as long as enough breeding stock remains to produce another crop of similar size the following year. Seasons for small game, waterfowl and upland birds are usually long and bag limits generous. Liberal regulations are possible, because of the high reproductive rates of these animals. Regulations for big game are stricter because the animals produce fewer young.

Resource agencies closely monitor game populations and set regulations to achieve the desired harvest. Modern management has virtually eliminated the problems of mass slaughter associated with market hunting in years past. In fact, some of the continent's major game species, such as white-tailed deer and wild turkey, are more numerous today than at any time in recorded history.

Factors That Affect Game Populations

174 Adult Grouse ———————————————— Predators and Disease Kill 24 Adults

174 Adults Produce 935 Eggs   Predators Destroy 374 Eggs   Predators and Disease Kill 337 Young

GAME POPULATIONS tend to remain stable if the habitat is not disturbed and hunting pressure is regulated. In a study of a ruffed grouse population in New York state, there were 174 adult grouse at the beginning of the breeding season. These birds produced 935 fertile eggs. As the months passed, 24 adult grouse succumbed to predators and disease, 26 to hunting, and 54 to severe weather. By the following spring, 70 birds remained to

BIG GAME POPULATIONS can reach high levels despite low reproductive rates. Predators take only an occasional young animal. In areas with good habitat and little hunting pressure, herds may grow so large that food shortages result. Hunting regulations are set to control the harvest, yet prevent overpopulation.

Hunters Take 26 Adults   Severe Weather Kills 54 Adults   70 Adults Survive

Hunters Take 38 Young   Severe Weather Kills 81 Young   105 Young Survive

breed again. Of the 935 eggs, 374 were destroyed by predators. The rest hatched, but 337 chicks were killed by predators and disease. Hunters claimed 38 of the young birds, 81 perished in winter storms, and 105 survived to the breeding season. These first-year breeders, combined with the 70 second-year birds, resulted in a total of 175 adult grouse, nearly identical to the breeding population of the previous year.

9

Senses of Game Animals

Game animals have an amazing ability to elude hunters. Their keen senses of sight, smell and hearing enable them to detect danger far in advance and take evasive action. Many animals also possess unique survival adaptations that far exceed the capabilities of humans.

Hunters who understand the senses and special adaptations of the game they pursue stand the best chance of success.

SIGHT. Game birds have color vision that may surpass that of humans. Their retinas have more color receptors, or *cones,* than most other game animals. Colored oil droplets in the retina work like a camera filter, enhancing the visibility of certain hues. The cones also give them excellent *visual acuity,* or sharpness.

Game mammals have retinas that contain mostly light receptors, or *rods.* The rods enable them to see well in dim light. The vision of most game mammals is not as sharp as that of birds or humans (see chart), and they have limited color vision, if any.

Most mammals have poor *accommodation* capabilities; they cannot change the shape of their lenses to focus on both close and distant objects. As a result, images are often fuzzy. This explains why many types of big game animals do not seem to notice a stationary hunter.

SMELL. Game mammals collect most of the information about their environment through their sense of smell. In a laboratory test, rabbits were able to detect the smell of acetone at a concentration of only 1/50th of that detectable by humans. Hunters who pursue big or small game should try to approach from downwind to keep their scent from drifting toward the animals.

Game birds have a poor sense of smell. In one study, wild turkey were given two piles of grain, one of which contained a highly repulsive scent. The birds paid no attention to the odor, feeding equally at each pile. To a bird in flight, a highly-developed sense of smell would be of little value because odors produced by predators quickly sink to the ground.

HEARING. Because birds lack external ears and because their ears have fewer small bones than those of mammals, they are not as well-equipped for detecting faint sounds. The range of pitches they can recognize is slightly less than that of humans, and substantially less than that of many game mammals.

In a test of their ability to detect various pitches, mallards recognized sounds up to a frequency of 8000 cycles per second (cps). Humans detected higher pitched sounds, up to 20,000 cps, and raccoon heard sounds of up to 85,000 cps.

SPECIAL ADAPTATIONS. The process of evolution has provided almost every type of game animal with some unique physical feature or ability that gives it an advantage over other animals. These adaptations enable the species to survive the threats posed by predators, including man.

Many of these adaptations are so foreign to humans that we fail to consider them when hunting. For example, a mallard can stay submerged for as long as 16 minutes. It accomplishes this seemingly impossible feat by slowing its heart rate by more than 50 percent while under water. This substantially reduces its oxygen needs.

Many a hunter has winged a duck, marked it down, spent 5 to 10 minutes looking for it, then given up in frustration. After the hunter returns to the blind, the duck appears in the very spot it went down.

COMMUNICATION is one way that animals alert each other to danger. Ducks and geese, for example, make alarm calls to warn other members of the flock. Animals use other vocal signals to rally their young after a predator attack, to mark their territories, to attract mates, and to intimidate other males during the breeding season.

Comparing the Senses of Man to Game Animals

	VISION	HEARING	SMELL
Man	Good	Good	Fair
White-tailed Deer	Fair	Excellent	Excellent
Cottontail Rabbit	Good	Excellent	Good
Wild Turkey	Excellent	Excellent	Poor
Ring-necked Pheasant	Good	Good	Poor
Mallard Duck	Excellent	Good	Fair

Adaptations Relating to Sight

COLOR VISION exists in some big game. In one study, white-tailed deer were rewarded with a drink from a tube when a red light went on; a white light gave no reward. Even though the lights switched between two tubes, deer consistently made the right choice.

NIGHT VISION in nocturnal animals is enhanced by the *Tapetum lucidum*, a layer of reflective pigment below the surface of the retina. Light passes through the receptors on the retina's surface, hits the tapetum, then bounces back to stimulate the receptors again.

Adaptations Relating to Hearing

INTERNAL EARS of birds do not collect sounds as efficiently as exposed ears. And because the ears are close together, they are not as well-suited to locating the direction of sounds.

EXPOSED EARS gather sound waves. They also help an animal pinpoint the source of a sound by the difference in the time it takes for the signal to reach each ear.

MOVABLE EARS enable mammals to locate sounds from any direction. While one ear detects a sound from one direction, the other picks up a sound from a different source.

Adaptations Relating to Smell

POSITIONING themselves below the crest of a wind-swept ridge enables some big game to smell anything approaching from above. They watch for anything coming from below.

SCENT GLANDS warn other animals of danger. When a mule deer faces a threat, *metatarsal glands* on the hind legs (arrow) produce an odor that alerts other herd members.

FREEZING in position and pressing its body to the ground reduces the amount of scent an animal gives off. Some game birds also compress their feathers so less scent escapes.

Other Special Adaptations

FLARED RUMP HAIR alerts other animals to a threat. By flaring its rump hairs to the side, the pronghorn can greatly increase the size and visibility of its white rump patch.

CAMOUFLAGE enables game animals to escape detection by predators. This woodcock blends in so well with the vegetation that it can hide in open terrain with no overhead cover.

GENETIC CHANGES may result from hunting. The tendency to run has increased among pheasants. Many hunters attribute this to the fact that fliers get shot, leaving runners to breed.

Wildlife Habitat

Good habitat is the key to wildlife abundance. Game animals need year-round cover and a reliable supply of food. Many also require drinking water on a regular basis, although some get sufficient water from their food or can go without for long periods.

The best wildlife habitat has a variety of plant life. A mixed plant community generally supports more species and higher numbers of game than an expanse of the same type of vegetation.

Most types of game find the necessary plant variety along the edge between two vegetative types. Where a forest meets a marsh, for instance, the mixture of grasses, berry bushes, low-growing leafy plants and young trees provide an excellent supply of food and cover. The area where the two types of vegetation meet usually holds more kinds and higher numbers of game than either type by itself. This principle is known as the *edge effect*.

Another factor that influences plant variety is *succession*. For example, after a forest fire or logging operation, the bare ground almost immediately begins to grow grasses, shrubs and trees. As the trees grow taller, they begin to form a *canopy* that shades the forest floor. As the canopy grows denser, shrubs and grasses disappear because of the lack of sunlight. Eventually, only large trees remain. These changes in the plant community invariably affect the type and amount of game the habitat can support.

Wildlife managers often set back the process of succession by periodically cutting or burning forested areas to promote growth of new vegetation. These techniques enable them to increase the production of important game species.

In most agricultural areas, the trend is toward less habitat variety. Many farms once had small, weedy cropfields combined with brushy fencelines, unmowed roadside ditches, large wetlands and dense groves. Today's clean farms have vast acreages of crops unbroken by fencelines, wetlands or trees. Even roadside ditches are often mowed for hay. These intensive agricultural practices severely reduce or eliminate populations of farmland game like pheasants and bobwhite quail.

How Succession Affects Game Populations

SUCCESSION begins after trees have been removed. New grasses, shrubs and trees (left) support animals like white-tailed deer. As time goes on, trees grow taller (middle), yet enough sunlight penetrates to promote a dense growth of underbrush ideal for animals like ruffed grouse. As the trees mature and shade out the forest floor (right), underbrush disappears and the forest becomes best suited for animals like black bear.

Where to Find Edge Habitat

FOREST CLEARINGS, like powerline corridors, logging roads, and logged or burned areas, usually hold more game than the forest interior. Marshes or grassy meadows in forests also attract wildlife.

FARMLANDS abutting forests or brushlands have an abundance of edge habitat. Ample sunlight reaches the forest or brushland margin, resulting in a lush growth of seed- and berry-producing plants.

MOUNTAIN SLOPES often have edge habitat where grassy foothills meet mid-elevation hardwoods; where hardwoods grade into high-elevation conifers; and at the treeline, where conifers end and lichens begin.

15

To many hunters, the term cover means a well-hidden spot where animals can escape danger. And it is true that escape cover is vital to the survival of almost every game species. But most wildlife also needs other kinds of cover for bedding, loafing, protection from the elements, and producing young.

A ring-necked pheasant, for example, often escapes from hunters by hiding in dense brush. It may roost in open grasslands, loaf along the grassy margin of a cropfield, and burrow under a clump of slough grass during a storm. Experienced hunters know where to look at different times of the day and under different weather conditions.

ESCAPE COVER. Predators pose a constant threat to most game animals. Wildlife must learn to contend with these threats, or perish. Most elude predators by hiding in dense cover; others scamper to a burrow or den; in light cover, some crouch motionless or rely on camouflage.

BEDDING COVER. Some game animals bed in dens or burrows, or roost in trees. Others prefer thick grassy cover for bedding sites. The grass offers concealment and warns animals of danger. Even the stealthiest predator would have difficulty moving through thick grass without making some noise.

LOAFING COVER. Most game animals feed heavily in early morning and late afternoon, then loaf during midday. Loafing cover is thick enough so that animals are not easily visible, but not so dense that they cannot see.

COVER FROM THE ELEMENTS. All game animals need some type of dense cover to insulate them from extremely cold temperatures. They also use cover as shelter from precipitation, strong winds and the hot summer sun.

Many birds and small mammals crawl under vegetation to escape harsh winter storms. Some burrow under the snow, creating a cozy enclosure. The animal's body heat may keep the temperature as much as 50 degrees warmer than the outside air. Big game animals may bed down under conifer limbs in a heavy rain or on a cold night. The boughs shed precipitation and act like a blanket to slow the loss of body heat into the atmosphere.

PRODUCTION COVER. Predators and adverse weather will quickly wipe out nesting adults and newly-produced young unless they have good production cover. This type of cover may not hold animals during the hunting season, but it often serves as an indicator of high game populations.

Examples of Basic Cover Types

THICKETS make good escape cover for almost every type of wild game. Brush breaks up the animal's outline and offers shade.

OPEN TIMBER is used as loafing cover by some types of big game. Small game and upland birds generally loaf in areas with denser ground cover.

ABANDONED BUILDINGS serve as windbreaks for many types of game. Old farmsteads often have dis-carded machinery, brush piles, tall weeds, and evergreen groves that offer cover from the elements.

TALL GRASS makes excellent bedding cover. It provides a comfortable resting spot and offers animals camouflage from predators.

MODERATELY DENSE VEGETATION provides nesting cover for many upland birds. They prefer cover open enough so they can see and escape if necessary.

Wildlife Habitat: Food and Water

Hunters who understand the feeding habits and water needs of their quarry can better predict its daily movements. This makes it easier to select a good hunting location.

An elk may travel miles to find food or quench its thirst, but most wildlife needs food and water in close proximity to cover. If an animal has to travel a long distance across open terrain to fulfill these basic needs, it is more visible to predators.

FOOD. Most game animals can adapt to a wide variety of foods. Researchers have found that bobwhite quail consume over 1000 different foods including seeds, plants, nuts and insects.

Despite their ability to use such a wide range of foods, most animals select items that they can digest easily and that are high in proteins and calories. They seem to instinctively know which foods are most nutritious. In one study, squirrels gained weight when fed a diet consisting solely of white oak acorns. But they lost weight when fed acorns of red oak. In nature, squirrels commonly feed on acorns of white oak, but ignore those of red oak.

Like humans, game animals must have vitamins and minerals in their diet. Most animals obtain these vital elements from their food and water, but some need additional salt. They frequent springs and natural soil deposits with high salt contents. Many birds pick up grit not only to grind their food, but to provide needed minerals.

WATER. Birds generally require less water than mammals, because they can reuse water as it passes through their digestive tract. Gambel's quail, for example, can go a month or two without visiting a water hole. Pronghorns, on the other hand, need water each day.

Many game species can survive in areas with no lakes, streams or other sources of surface water. They obtain water from foods or dew.

Sources of Wildlife Food

NATURAL FOODS are the mainstay in the diets of most game animals. A good supply of winter food is especially critical. Survival rates are generally low in years when winter food is scarce.

FOOD PLOTS planted by wildlife agencies provide an additional source of food during winter, when natural food may be difficult to find. Some farmers leave a few rows of corn to sustain wildlife on their land.

WASTE GRAIN remains after farmers harvest their crops. It provides a temporary food supply for many animals like geese, ducks, pheasants and deer. They gather in large numbers to take advantage of this easy source of food. Waste grain may provide food throughout the winter where fields are left unplowed.

Sources of Water

SURFACE WATER is a requirement for many kinds of game. Popular watering sites include streams, lakes, man-made ponds and natural springs.

SUCCULENT FOODS, like prickly-pear cactus, provide water in arid climates. Rabbits and grouse often get water from grasses and buds.

FROST OR DEW also provides water in dry climates. To use this water source, animals must feed in early morning before the plants dry off.

Wildlife Habitat: Common Types

Some game animals can adapt to almost any kind of habitat. White-tailed deer, for instance, live in places as diverse as Florida swamps, southwestern deserts, and mountains of the Pacific Northwest. But most types of wildlife have much more specific habitat requirements.

When hunting in unfamiliar territory, it pays to spend a good deal of time scouting. Conditions may not be right for spotting game, but you can always recognize good habitat.

Many types of wildlife have cover, food or water needs so specific that merely finding a broad habitat type is not enough. For example, moose prefer young conifer-hardwood forests. But within these forests, they seldom stray far from streambanks, lakeshores or willow bogs, their main feeding sites. Sage grouse live in semi-arid brushlands, but rarely venture more than one-half mile from a water hole or other source of water.

GRASSLANDS usually have grasses growing in combination with broad-leaved green plants, or *forbs*. The height of the vegetation varies from less than 18 inches in arid habitats to 10 feet where the soil is moist.

BRUSHLANDS have shrubs mixed with grasses and forbs; some have widely-spaced trees. The vegetation may be so thick that it is impenetrable. Brushlands are often an intermediate stage between grassland and forest.

MIXED FORESTS have a blend of conifers and hardwoods. The combination of a good food supply and abundant cover enables these forests to produce more wildlife than coniferous or deciduous forests alone.

SEMI-ARID DESERTS contain shrubs, grasses and cactuses, and may have some trees. They support more types of game than arid deserts, which have only scattered shrubs and cactuses.

As the seasons change, many species of game migrate to different types of habitat. In late fall, waterfowl leave northern marshes en masse. Most winter in the South, resting and feeding on large lakes and in cropfields. As winter approaches, some types of mountain wildlife migrate to lower elevations, wintering in grasslands that offer more food and a less severe climate.

Hunting pressure may also force animals from their preferred habitat. Elk favor grassy mountain meadows, but when hunters begin to invade their territory, they retreat to higher, more rugged terrain where a man on foot could not follow. Waterfowl abandon many small lakes and ponds once the season opens. They seek refuge in the open water of large lakes and reservoirs.

In agricultural areas, wildlife may have to use other cover once crops are harvested. Pheasant hunters usually find the birds in cropfields during early season. But when the crops are removed, the birds move to permanent heavy cover like cattail swamps and woodlots.

Throughout this book, we will identify the habitats most commonly associated with each species of game. Following are the major habitat types to which we will refer.

DECIDUOUS FORESTS, also called *hardwood forests,* contain trees that lose their leaves in fall. The leaves rot quickly, forming rich humus. Buds, nuts, shrubs and green plants provide food for wildlife.

CONIFEROUS FORESTS have dense stands of needle- or scale-leaved evergreen trees that provide some cover. Leaves that fall to the ground decompose slowly, forming acidic soil which produces few wildlife foods.

WETLANDS have pockets of open water and dense stands of emergent vegetation like cattails and cane. The open water produces food for waterfowl and the fringes provide cover for a wide variety of game.

AGRICULTURAL LANDS with a variety of cover types support a diversity of wildlife. The fertile soil produces abundant food and larger animals than most other types of habitat.

Skills and Equipment

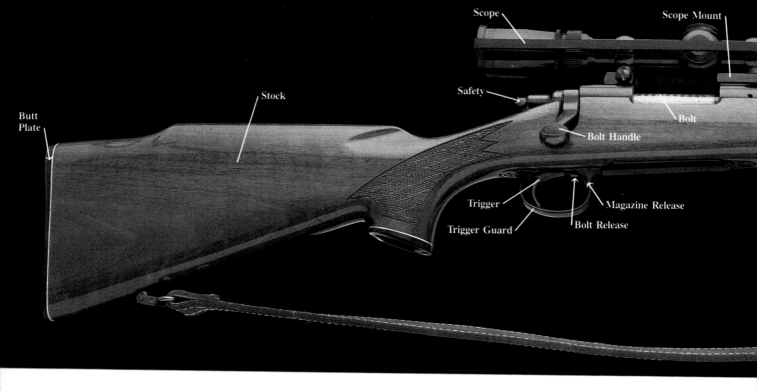

Butt
Plate

Stock

Scope

Scope Mount

Safety

Bolt

Bolt Handle

Trigger

Magazine Release

Trigger Guard

Bolt Release

The Hunting Rifle

A rifle that suits your style of hunting greatly increases your chances of success. When selecting a rifle, consider its action, weight and caliber.

ACTION. The action refers to the design of the mechanism for chambering ammunition and ejecting spent cartridges. Single-shot actions, like the *falling block,* are extremely reliable because they have few moving parts. Their rigid mechanisms hold the cartridge firmly, resulting in a high degree of accuracy. These rifles must be reloaded after each

round is fired, so they teach shooters to make the first shot count.

Repeating actions hold several cartridges in the magazine, making it possible to fire more than one shot without reloading. Like single shots, *bolt* actions have a rigid design and few moving parts. Many hunters consider the bolt action to be the most accurate and reliable rifle. *Lever, pump* and *semi-automatic* actions are designed for faster firing. You may need a quick second shot if you fail to kill the animal or if a branch deflects your bullet. But fast-action rifles have more moving parts, increasing the chance of mechanical failure, especially in cold weather or when dirt gets into the action.

WEIGHT. Rifles commonly weigh between 6 and 9 pounds without cartridges, slings or scopes. The recoil, or *kick,* of a rifle depends mainly on its

POPULAR ACTIONS include: (1) falling block and (2) lever actions, which chamber and eject cartridges by means of a lever under the trigger guard; (3) bolt action, in which the cartridge locks in place by moving the bolt forward and downward, much like a door bolt; (4) pump

or *slide* action, which chambers and ejects by sliding the forearm back and forth; (5) semi-automatic or *autoloader* action, which chambers and ejects cartridges automatically after each shot. The action is powered by gases from the burning powder or by the recoil.

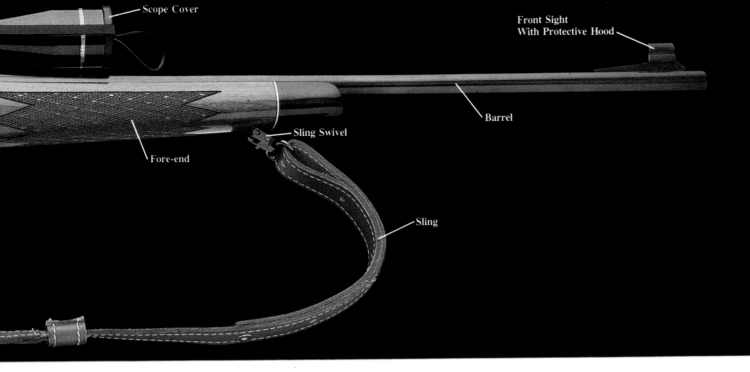

Scope Cover

Front Sight
With Protective Hood

Barrel

Sling Swivel

Fore-end

Sling

weight. A heavy rifle has the least recoil, because the weight absorbs much of the energy that would otherwise be transmitted to your shoulder. Heavy rifles are easiest to hold steady and generally result in more accurate shots. Light rifles are easier to carry over a long distance.

The term *carbine* denotes a light rifle with a short barrel. Many hunters prefer carbines when hunting in heavy cover, where a longer rifle would tend to catch on brush or tree limbs.

CALIBER. The caliber of a rifle refers to the diameter of the barrel opening, or *bore*. Caliber is measured in hundredths or thousandths of an inch, or in millimeters. Hunters use rifles as small as .17 caliber for small animals and rifles up to .458 caliber for big game. Many rifle models are available in a choice of several calibers. The Ruger Model M-77®,

for example, is a bolt action that comes in 15 different calibers.

Hunters are often confused by traditional caliber designations. A .30-06 rifle has a .30-inch diameter bore. The 06 refers to 1906, the year the rifle was introduced. A .30-30 rifle also shoots a .30 caliber bullet. The bullet was originally propelled by 30 grains of smokeless powder. To further complicate the matter, some caliber designations do not refer to the diameter of the bore. For example, the bore of a .308 Winchester rifle does not measure .308 inch. The .308 refers to the *groove diameter,* or the diameter to the outside of the *rifling grooves*. The bore diameter is only .30 inch.

Refer to the ammunition section (pages 26-27) for more information on selecting the best caliber for the game you hunt.

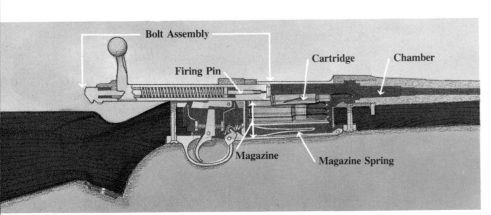

Bolt Assembly

Firing Pin

Cartridge

Chamber

Magazine

Magazine Spring

THE RECEIVER contains the working parts of a rifle. With a bolt-action, a spring forces a cartridge out of the magazine when the bolt is drawn back. When pushed forward, the bolt seats a cartridge in the chamber. Pulling the trigger causes the firing pin to strike the cartridge primer, igniting the powder. Drawing the bolt back extracts the spent cartridge.

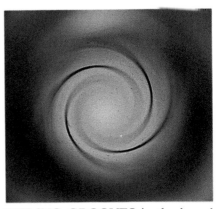

RIFLING GROOVES in the barrel cause the bullet to spin rapidly. The spinning motion makes the bullet travel smoothly without wobbling, much like a spiraling football.

25

Rifle Ammunition

Your choice of ammunition depends mainly on the size of the animal you hunt and the distance at which you do most of your shooting.

A bullet's hitting power is determined by its weight and velocity. The heavier and faster the bullet, the more energy it delivers to the target. At normal shooting ranges, a light, fast bullet generally delivers as much energy and kills as effectively as a heavier but slower bullet. Hitting power is measured in *foot-pounds*.

The *trajectory*, or flight path, of a bullet also depends on its velocity. A fast bullet has a flat trajectory, so you do not have to compensate as much for bullet drop at long ranges.

Most hunters use small, low-velocity cartridges for short-range shooting at small game like rabbits and squirrels. For long-range shooting at animals up to the size of pronghorn or mule deer, they use medium caliber, high-velocity cartridges. Larger caliber, high-velocity cartridges work best for long-range shooting at bigger animals like elk or moose.

Many hunters prefer medium and large caliber, low-velocity cartridges, like the .30-30, for hunting big game animals in heavy brush. They believe that these cartridges are less likely to deflect when they hit twigs or saplings. But ballistics tests have shown that low-velocity cartridges actually deflect more than high-velocity cartridges.

To determine the ammunition best-suited for the game you hunt, consult a *ballistics table*. Most ammunition catalogs contain ballistics information including bullet energy and drop at different ranges. Some hunters memorize the drop figures for their cartridge or tape the numbers to their rifle stock.

When selecting cartridges, hunters should consider *load*, or the bullet weight and strength of the powder charge. Magnum loads generally have stonger powder charges than standard loads. But some manufacturers misuse the term. A true magnum has a flatter trajectory and more hitting power than a standard cartridge of the same caliber and bullet weight. Check a ballistics table to be sure that a cartridge is truly a magnum.

The shape and construction of a bullet also affects its trajectory and hitting power. A long, thin, streamlined bullet retains its velocity at longer ranges than a short, stout bullet. So the longer bullet has a flatter trajectory. A properly constructed bullet will *mushroom* when it hits and will not break apart. So, all of the bullet's energy is expended in the target.

Two rifles with the same caliber bore may require different cartridges. A .30-30 cartridge, for example, will not substitute for a .30-06 cartridge, even though both bullets measure .30 inches in diameter. The .30-06 has a larger case and will not fit in a .30-30 chamber.

Never use ammunition other than that recommended for your rifle by the manufacturer. The result could be a damaged rifle and serious injury.

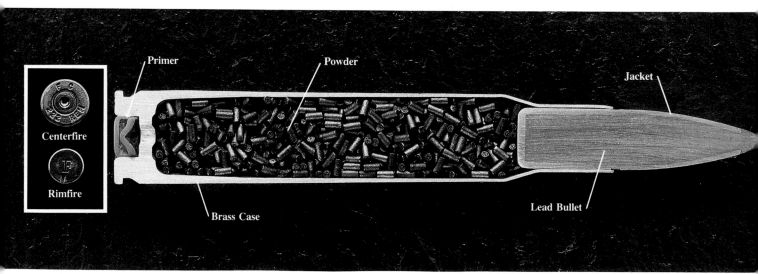

CENTERFIRE cartridges consist of: a brass case; a primer containing a highly explosive compound that ignites when struck by the firing pin; powder, which is ignited by the priming compound; a lead bullet, which may have a copper-zinc jacket to control the bullet's expansion. The inset shows spent centerfire and rimfire cases. With rimfires, the firing pin strikes the edge of the rim, igniting the priming compound.

BULLET STYLES include (1) *pointed,* streamlined for high velocity and flat trajectory. (2) *Pointed boat tail* has a tapered base to reduce drag even more. (3) *Hollow* points mushroom rapidly, but no faster than (4) *flat* and (5) *round* points, often used in rifles with tubular magazines. Their blunt points will not detonate cartridges ahead of them, but result in relatively slow flight and short range. (6) Mushroomed round point shows maximum expansion. (7) *Nosler™ partition* (cross-section) has a thin-walled front core and thick-walled rear core. (8) Mushroomed Nosler™ shows expansion in front, but the rear core keeps it shape.

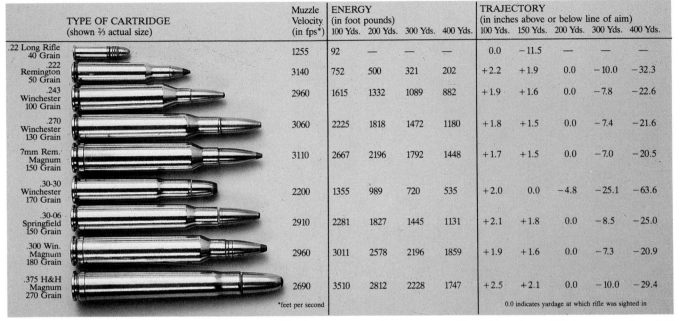

TYPE OF CARTRIDGE (shown ⅔ actual size)	Muzzle Velocity (in fps*)	ENERGY (in foot pounds)				TRAJECTORY (in inches above or below line of aim)				
		100 Yds.	200 Yds.	300 Yds.	400 Yds.	100 Yds.	150 Yds.	200 Yds.	300 Yds.	400 Yds.
.22 Long Rifle 40 Grain	1255	92	—	—	—	0.0	−11.5	—	—	—
.222 Remington 50 Grain	3140	752	500	321	202	+2.2	+1.9	0.0	−10.0	−32.3
.243 Winchester 100 Grain	2960	1615	1332	1089	882	+1.9	+1.6	0.0	−7.8	−22.6
.270 Winchester 130 Grain	3060	2225	1818	1472	1180	+1.8	+1.5	0.0	−7.4	−21.6
7mm Rem. Magnum 150 Grain	3110	2667	2196	1792	1448	+1.7	+1.5	0.0	−7.0	−20.5
.30-30 Winchester 170 Grain	2200	1355	989	720	535	+2.0	0.0	−4.8	−25.1	−63.6
.30-06 Springfield 150 Grain	2910	2281	1827	1445	1131	+2.1	+1.8	0.0	−8.5	−25.0
.300 Win. Magnum 180 Grain	2960	3011	2578	2196	1859	+1.9	+1.6	0.0	−7.3	−20.9
.375 H&H Magnum 270 Grain	2690	3510	2812	2228	1747	+2.5	+2.1	0.0	−10.0	−29.4

*feet per second

0.0 indicates yardage at which rifle was sighted in

BALLISTICS TABLES help you determine the effective killing range of your cartridge, and bullet drop at various ranges. This table lists muzzle velocity, and the energy in foot-pounds delivered at ranges from 100 to 400 yards. As a rule, use a cartridge with at least 900 foot-pounds to kill a deer, 1500 for an elk and 2100 for a moose. Trajectory figures show how far the bullet strikes above (+) or below (−) the point of aim at ranges from 100 to 400 yards.

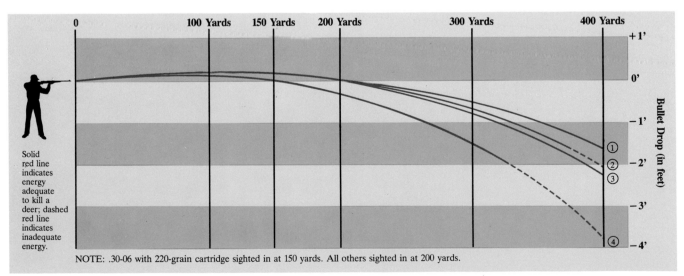

NOTE: .30-06 with 220-grain cartridge sighted in at 150 yards. All others sighted in at 200 yards.

LOAD affects trajectory and energy. This chart compares four, .30 caliber bullets: (1) a 180-grain .300 Winchester Magnum; and (2) 150, (3) 180 and (4) 220-grain .30-06 bullets. The 180-grain .300 magnum has a flatter trajectory than the 180-grain .30-06. The 180-grain .30-06 retains energy longer but drops more than the 150-grain .30-06. The 220-grain .30-06 has the lowest velocity, so it drops most and has the shortest effective range.

27

Rifle Sights

Even the best rifle is of little use without an accurate sighting device. Some hunters spend as much for a telescopic sight as for the rifle itself.

Most rifles come with iron sights. To aim, the hunter centers a post at the end of the barrel in a notch or peep-hole in the rear sight. Iron sights are inexpensive, lightweight, durable and best-suited for short-range shooting.

For long-range shooting in open country, most hunters prefer telescopic sights, or *scopes*. A scope consists of a metal tube containing a system of lenses to magnify the target. The *reticle*, a network of lines or crosshairs, enables you to aim precisely. The optics allow you to focus your eye on the reticle and target at the same time, so you can aim quickly. Scopes are not as durable as iron sights and are easier to knock out of adjustment.

Scopes vary in magnification power, from 1.5x, which magnifies the target 1½ times, to 12x. Most hunters use scopes ranging in power from 2x to 9x. Low-power scopes work best for close-range shooting. They allow you to view a large area, making it easy to find your target. High-power scopes narrow the field of view, but help you see a distant animal.

Most manufacturers offer a selection of special purpose scopes. Variable power scopes enable you to adjust the magnification. *Rangefinder* scopes help you estimate the shooting range; some have adjustments to compensate for bullet drop.

4-PLEX™ reticles have wires that are thick toward the outside. These wires stand out against the background and draw your eye to the target. The thin crosshairs enable you to aim precisely, without obscuring the animal.

Other Types of Sights and Scopes

OPEN sights have a blade or post, which must be centered in the notched rear sight. They are the most difficult of the sights to align, and the rear sight covers up part of the target.

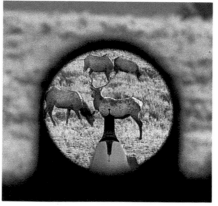

PEEP sights require you to center the target in a hole in the rear sight, then place the bead directly on the animal. Hunters prefer large peep-holes so they can see most of the target.

CROSSHAIR reticles work best for long-range shooting. The fine wires provide a precise aiming point and cover little of the target. But the wires may be difficult to see in dim light.

How to Use a Variable Power Scope

TURN the adjustment ring on a variable power scope to change the magnification. Common power ranges are 1.5x to 4.5x, 2x to 7x, and 3x to 9x.

KEEP a variable scope on low power in most situations. At 3x power, for example, you can easily find and center the animal in the scope.

INCREASE the power for long-range shooting at standing game. At 9x, the same animal nearly fills the scope, making it easier to aim.

How to Use a Rangefinder Scope (for Deer)

ADJUST the power until the animal's body just fits between the top two wires. Read the distance (300 yards) at the bottom of the scale.

SET the elevation dial to the same range to adjust for bullet drop. Refer to the owner's manual to set the dial for larger or smaller game.

ZOOM IN to aim at the animal. Hold the crosshairs directly on the target. The bullet should strike near the point of aim without holding high.

DOT reticles feature a small dot that keeps your eye on the center of the crosshairs. They work best for short-range shooting; at long ranges, the dot obscures much of the target.

POST reticles have a thick post that stands out against dense timber or brush, and works well for tracking a moving target. At long range, the post may cover some of the target.

WIDE-ANGLE scopes provide a wide field of view. Because you can see more terrain, you can spot animals more quickly. Wide-angle scopes enable you to follow running game.

Sighting In Your Rifle

Many a hunter has lost his chance for a trophy because of a rifle that was not sighted in. Before hunting, sight in any new rifle or one that has been handled roughly.

You can sight in most easily at a shooting range. Most ranges have bench rests and sandbags to provide a steady rest and minimize human error. If sighting in your rifle in the field, make sure you shoot into a solid backstop.

To shoot accurately, take a deep breath, exhale halfway, then hold your breath as you squeeze the trigger. Do not jerk the trigger as you shoot.

Sights on a new rifle may be so far out of adjustment that you will miss the target completely. To solve this problem, *rough sight* your rifle at close range, generally about 25 yards. One method, termed *bore sighting,* involves sighting through the opening in the barrel. Look directly through the bore of a bolt or falling block action. You cannot look directly through the bore of most other actions, so you must use a bore-sighting tool.

You can also rough-sight your rifle by simply aiming at a close target through the sights, firing, then making any adjustments needed to hit the bullseye.

Once you have rough-sighted at 25 yards, back off to 100 yards. Continue to fine-tune the sights until you can center the shot group on the bullseye. If you plan to shoot at longer ranges, sight in a few inches high at 100 yards. Then try a few long-range shots and make any necessary adjustments.

Always hunt with the same type of ammunition you used to sight in. Changing brands or bullet weights often makes it necessary to realign your sights.

How to Rough-sight a Rifle

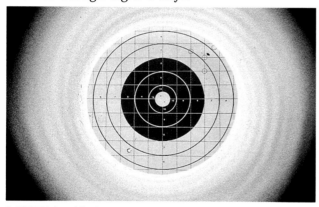

MOVE the rifle barrel until the center of the bore lines up with the bullseye of a target 25 yards away. Fix the rifle's position so it cannot move, then adjust the sights to aim at the bullseye.

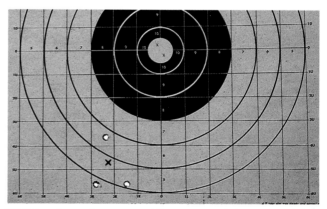

FIRE a three-shot group. The center of the group (X) is the average point of impact. If the center is not in the bullseye, adjust the sights. It may take several three-shot groups to zero in.

How to Adjust Rifle Sights

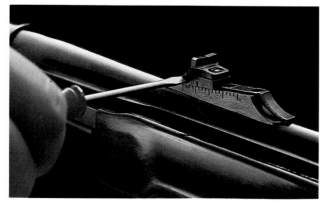

ADJUST iron sights by moving the rear sight in the direction you want the rifle to shoot. To make the rifle shoot higher, raise the rear sight. To make it shoot to the left, move the rear sight to the left.

CENTER telescopic sights by turning the adjuster screws. For most scopes, moving the adjuster screw one mark changes the point of impact 1 inch at 100 yards. Refer to your owner's manual for precise instructions.

STEADY your rifle on a sandbag atop a bench rest when sighting in. Hold the stock firmly against your shoulder.

Protect your eyes and ears with shooting glasses and ear muffs. Use a spotting scope to check the target.

How to Sight In for Long Distance Shooting

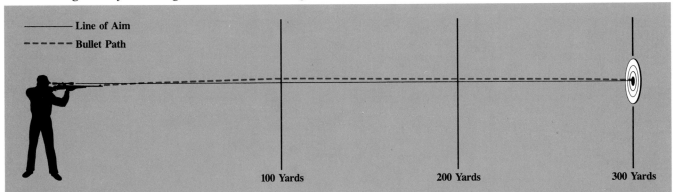

——— Line of Aim

- - - - Bullet Path

100 Yards   200 Yards   300 Yards

SIGHT IN your rifle so the bullet hits just above the point of aim at 100 yards. For most flat-shooting cartridges, you should zero in 2 to 3 inches high; the exact distance depends on the trajectory of your bullet. By sighting in this way, you can aim dead-on at your target at any range up to 300 yards. The bullet will hit slightly high or low, depending on the range, but will strike somewhere in the animal's vital area.

Tips for Sighting In Your Rifle

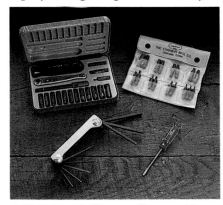

CARRY tools like small screwdrivers and hex keys to adjust iron sights, to turn scope adjuster screws and to tighten scope mounting screws.

MAKE a bullseye with several 1-inch squares of black tape. The squares make it easy to judge the distance between a bullet hole and the bullseye.

REST the forearm of your rifle on a sandbag or folded jacket on your vehicle. Use a spotting scope to see bullet holes in the target.

Shooting a Rifle

Shooting a rifle under hunting conditions is more difficult than shooting at a target range. To shoot accurately, hunters must assume a stable position, and know how to compensate for wind, uphill or downhill angles, and moving animals.

Whenever possible, try to find a stable object to provide a steady rest for your rifle. If you cannot find such an object, the prone position is your next best choice. But shooting from the prone position may be impossible if ground cover or rolling terrain obscures your line of sight. Under these conditions, most hunters use the sitting position, which offers good stability because both elbows rest on the knees. The kneeling position is less stable, because only one elbow rests on the knee. The offhand position is the least stable. However, it may be the only choice when a moving animal offers a brief chance for a shot.

Hunters should learn how to adjust for natural forces like *wind drift* and the *slant range effect*. A strong crosswind dramatically affects a bullet's flight path. To hit a standing target, you must compensate by aiming slightly upwind.

The slant range effect causes your bullet to hit high whenever you shoot uphill or downhill. This confusing phenomenon results from the fact that gravity acts at a right angle to the horizontal. When a bullet is shot on a horizontal plane, gravity pulls at a right angle over the entire distance to the target, resulting in a curved flight path. But when a bullet is shot vertically, either straight up or straight down, gravity does not bend the flight path at all. The closer the angle to the vertical, the less the flight path curves.

A rifle is usually sighted in on the horizontal, so the sights are adjusted to compensate for maximum bullet drop. Since the bullet does not drop as much when shooting uphill or downhill, it always hits high. To compensate, aim low.

Most hunters tend to shoot behind running animals. A hunter using 150-grain .30-06 bullets would maintain a 4- to 5-foot lead at a deer running at a right angle 100 yards away. At 200 yards, he would increase the lead to about 10 feet and at 300 yards, to about 16 feet.

Practice your lead by shooting at a rolling tire with a cardboard target wedged inside. Position yourself on a hill, then have someone roll the tire past you.

SITTING. If you shoot right-handed, sit with your legs about 30 degrees to the right of your line of aim and rest your elbows firmly on your knees. Sitting is the most useful shooting position. You can use the position almost anywhere, assume it quickly and shoot accurately.

PRONE. Lie with your body about 30 degrees left of your line of aim. Place your left elbow just left of the rifle. Pull your right leg forward to lift your stomach off the ground, so your breathing does not affect the shot.

KNEELING. Sit on your right foot with your body 45 degrees left of the line of aim. Place your left foot forward and your left elbow on the knee.

OFFHAND. Stand sideways with feet parallel to the line of aim. Spread your legs to shoulder width. Keep your left elbow close to your body.

SOLID REST. Rest your left hand or elbow on a solid object, like a tree or rock. Do not rest your rifle directly on the object.

Factors That Affect a Bullet's Flight Path

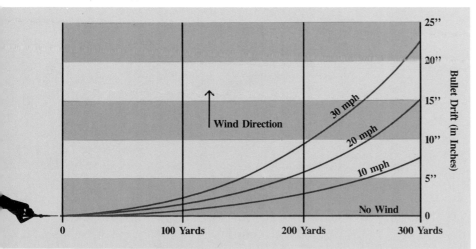

WIND DRIFT increases as wind velocity and range increase. The chart shows how crosswinds of 10, 20 and 30 mph would affect the path of a .30-06, 150-grain bullet at 100, 200 and 300 yards. As the chart indicates, a 10 mph crosswind would cause the bullet to drift less than 1 inch at 100 yards. But in a 30 mph crosswind, the bullet would drift over 22 inches at 300 yards.

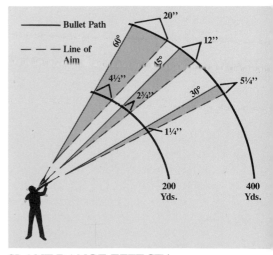

SLANT RANGE EFFECT increases with distance and angle. A 200-yard shot at 30 degrees hits about 1 inch higher than normal. A 400-yard shot at 60 degrees hits 20 inches higher.

33

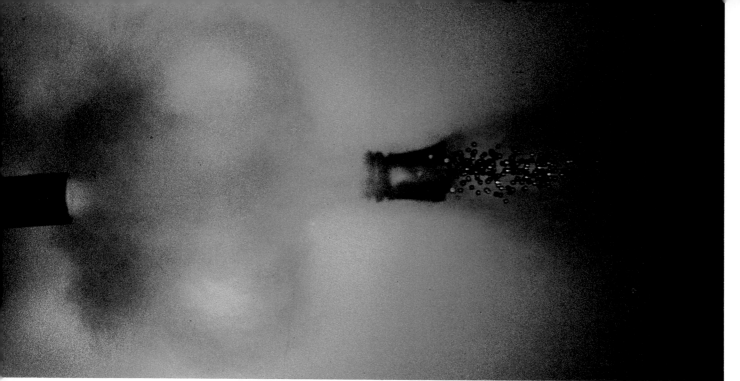

PELLETS leave the muzzle at about 1200 feet per second when a shotgun is discharged. Most shells contain a plastic wad that encases the shot and reduces deformation of the pellets as they pass down the barrel. The rear of the plastic wad acts as a gas sealant and further reduces shot deformation by absorbing much of the impact of the blast.

Shotguns

Frontiersmen referred to the shotgun as a *scatter-gun* because it sprayed a swarm of lead pellets. A shot swarm is more effective than a single bullet for hitting moving targets.

When selecting a shotgun, consider the following: size of the bore; *choke*, or amount of barrel constriction; action; chamber length; weight; and barrel type.

BORE SIZE. Shotgun bores are measured in gauge or in inches. As gauge increases, the size of the bore decreases. The most common gauges are 12 and 20, but gauges range from as small as 28 to as large as 10. The smallest bore is the .410, the only bore measured in inches. The larger the bore, the more pellets a gun can shoot. The denser *shot pattern* increases the chances for a long-range kill.

CHOKE. The choke also affects shot pattern. A barrel that narrows toward the end will shoot a tighter pattern than one with no constriction. A *full* choke constricts the barrel more than a *modified* choke. An *improved cylinder* has only slightly more constriction than a barrel with no choke. The best choke depends on your average shooting distance. For close-range shooting, an open choke like the improved cylinder works well. At longer range, a full choke puts more shot in the target.

Double-barreled shotguns usually have a different choke in each barrel. The second barrel has a tighter choke than the first to increase your chances of hitting game as it moves farther away.

Many guns have interchangeable barrels, each with a different choke. Some hunters install adjustable chokes at the end of the barrel. Screw-in chokes fit inside the muzzle.

ACTION. Most single-shot and double-barreled shotguns have a *hinge* action. The simple hinge design is more reliable than repeating actions, like the pump and semi-automatic. Pump shotguns are more dependable than semi-automatics, which may malfunction in cold weather.

CHAMBER LENGTH. Most shotguns are chambered for standard-load shells. To shoot many types of magnum loads, you need a gun with a longer chamber. The proper shell length is usually engraved on the barrel. Never shoot a shell that exceeds that length.

WEIGHT. A light shotgun works best for quick shots in heavy cover. When you have more time to shoot, a heavier gun works better. You can hold the barrel steadier and swing on a target more smoothly.

BARREL TYPE. A long barrel gives you a long sighting plane and can improve your shooting accuracy. But contrary to popular belief, a longer barrel does not mean a tighter choke. Nor does it noticeably increase shooting range.

Many guns come with *ventilated ribs*. A rib makes it easier to sight down the barrel and cools the barrel quickly, an advantage for rapid-fire shooting.

SHOTGUNS come in three barrel configurations: (1) side-by-side, (2) over-and-under, (3) single-barrel. Some over-and-unders, called *combination guns,* have a rifle barrel on top and a shotgun barrel below.

How Choke Affects the Shot Pattern

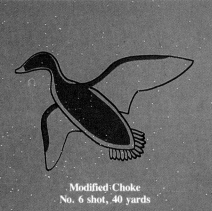

Improved Cylinder Choke
No. 6 shot, 40 yards

Modified Choke
No. 6 shot, 40 yards

Full Choke
No. 6 shot, 40 yards

CHOKE determines how quickly your shot spreads. With a 12 gauge, improved cylinder choke and a standard-load No. 6 shell, about 13 pellets hit the vulnerable area (red) of a stationary mallard silhouette at 40 yards. With a modified choke, about 16 pellets strike the target and with a full choke, about 20. Fewer pellets would strike a flying bird, because not all pellets in the shot swarm reach the target at the same time.

Shotgun Tips

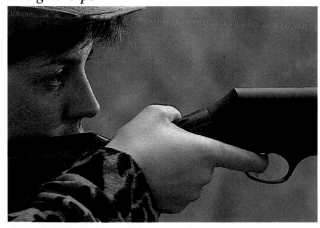

PROPER FIT should be checked while wearing your hunting clothes. You should be able to bring the gun to your shoulder in one motion, without the butt catching on your clothing. When you point the gun, the heel of your thumb should be 2 to 3 inches from your nose.

SCREW-IN CHOKES enable you to change your shot pattern for different types of hunting. These chokes screw into the barrel, so they have little effect on the gun's appearance. Use a specially-designed wrench to install and remove the chokes.

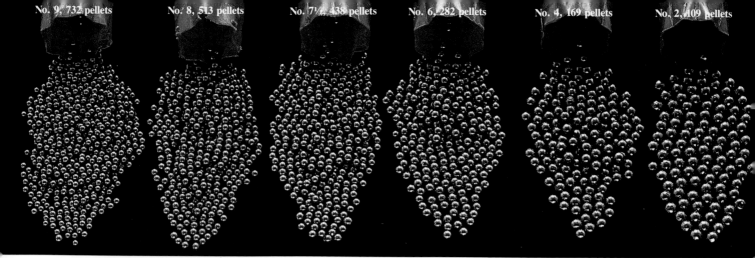

No. 9, 732 pellets   No. 8, 513 pellets   No. 7½, 438 pellets   No. 6, 282 pellets   No. 4, 169 pellets   No. 2, 109 pellets

POPULAR SHOT SIZES vary from No. 9 to 000 Buck. Nos. 9, 8 and 7½ are used mainly for small birds. Sizes 6 to 4 work best for medium-sized birds like ducks and

pheasants, for small game and for head shots at wild turkeys. Goose hunters generally use shot sizes between No. 4 and No. 4 Buckshot, but No. 6 shot will work at

Shotgun Shells

Choosing shotgun shells is much like selecting rifle cartridges. You must consider the size of the game you hunt and the distance at which you normally shoot.

Size of the animal usually determines the size of shot. Hunters prefer small shot for small animals. It penetrates deep enough to kill, but does not damage too much meat. Larger shot would obviously kill a small animal, but the chances of missing it are

greater. Shells with larger shot have fewer pellets, resulting in more open space in the pattern.

Large shot retains energy longer, so it carries farther and penetrates better than small shot. But very large shot is not necessarily better for long-range shooting. Use the largest shot that still has a sufficiently dense pattern at your usual shooting distance.

Load, or weight of the shot and strength of the powder charge, will also affect your shooting range. *Field* loads have the least shot and weakest powder charge with increasing charges in *standard* and *mag-*

SHOTGUN SHELLS vary in size from a standard .410 to a 10 gauge magnum. With No. 4 shot, a (1) standard .410 shell contains about 67 pellets; (2) a standard 28 gauge, 101; (3) a standard 20 gauge, 135; (4) a standard 16 gauge, 152; (5) a standard 12 gauge, 169; (6) a 10 gauge, 3½-inch magnum, 270. Larger shells do not necessarily have longer ranges. But because they contain more shot, they provide a denser shot pattern.

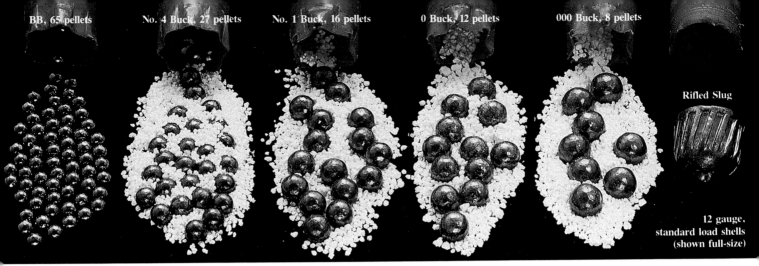

BB, 65 pellets   No. 4 Buck, 27 pellets   No. 1 Buck, 16 pellets   0 Buck, 12 pellets   000 Buck, 8 pellets

Rifled Slug

12 gauge,
standard load shells
(shown full-size)

close range. In the South, hunters use No. 1 Buckshot to 000 Buckshot for deer. Most states allow deer hunters to use rifled slugs. Plastic buffering material, shown in the

shells with large shot, keeps the pattern tighter. The buffer cushions the shot, so the pellets are less likely to flatten out and fly erratically.

num loads. For example, 12 gauge, 2¾-inch shells come in field loads that contain 1⅛ ounces of shot and 3¼ dram equivalents of powder; standard loads with 1¼ ounces of shot and 3¾ dr. equivs. of powder; and magnum loads with 1½ ounces of shot and 3¾ dr. equivs. of powder.

Field loads are adequate for close-range shooting at squirrels and rabbits, and for small to medium-sized birds. Standard loads work better at longer ranges, and for larger animals. Many hunters believe that magnum loads greatly increase their shooting range.

But a magnum of the same length as a standard load may actually have a slightly lower velocity and a shorter range. The advantage of a magnum is a denser shot pattern.

Some magnum shells have longer cases that hold even more shot and powder. A 12 gauge, 3-inch magnum, for example, contains 1⅞ ounces of shot and 4 dr. equivs. of powder. Its effective range is about 10 yards longer than a standard 2¾-inch load. Never attempt to shoot a long-cased magnum shell in a gun chambered for standard shells.

How Pellet Size Affects Shot Pattern

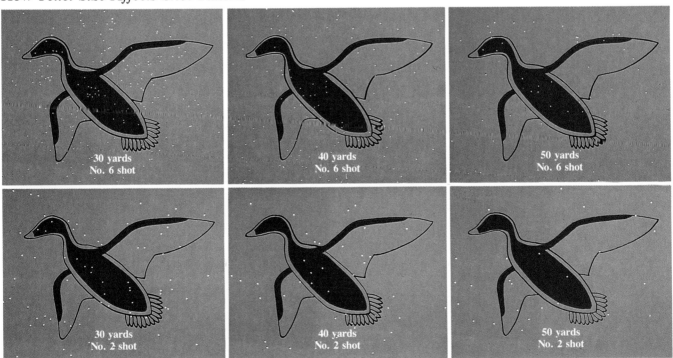

30 yards
No. 6 shot

40 yards
No. 6 shot

50 yards
No. 6 shot

30 yards
No. 2 shot

40 yards
No. 2 shot

50 yards
No. 2 shot

SHOT PATTERN depends on pellet size and the choke of your barrel. The top row shows patterns for a modified choke with a standard 12 gauge shell and No. 6 shot. About 34 pellets strike the vulnerable area (red) of a stationary mallard silhouette at 30 yards, about 16 pellets at 40 yards, and 12 at 50 yards. With No. 2 shot and the same choke (bottom), about 13 pellets hit the mallard target at 30 yards, about 5 at 40 yards, and 2 at 50 yards.

Shooting a Shotgun

Expert shotgunners develop their skills through practice. It takes little skill to hit a standing target with a shotgun, but moving game is a challenge. You must adjust for different angles, ranges and flight speeds, all within seconds.

Because a moving animal offers only a brief opportunity for a shot, you must learn to mount the gun quickly and consistently. Place the butt against your shoulder and press your cheek against the stock. Keep both eyes open and sight down the barrel with your dominant eye, which for most right-handed shooters is the right eye.

Practice mounting the gun and operating the safety at home. Wear your hunting coat, and make sure

The Swing-through Technique

START your swing with the barrel behind the bird. Move the barrel smoothly and steadily, so it starts to catch up with the bird's tail.

CONTINUE swinging so the barrel moves ahead of the bird. How far ahead depends on the distance, and the speed and angle of the bird's flight.

Other Shooting Techniques

SNAP-SHOOTING is the most effective technique for quick shots at crossing or straight-away targets at close range. Simply shoot at the point where you think the bird will be when the shot arrives.

SUSTAINED-LEAD shooting works well when a long-range target offers ample time to aim. Determine your lead, hold the barrel that far ahead of the bird, and pull the trigger while maintaining your lead.

that you can bring the gun to your shoulder without it catching on your clothing. Quickly draw a bead on stationary objects. Rotate your shoulders and hips as if following a moving target. Be sure your shotgun is unloaded before you practice.

Shotgunners use three basic techniques for moving game. *Snap-shooting* works well at close range. But for crossing targets at longer distances, use the *swing-through* or *sustained-lead* methods.

To sharpen your accuracy, shoot at practice targets, or *clay pigeons*. Practice at a shooting range or have a friend throw clay pigeons with a *hand trap*. Fire at crossing, overhead and straight-away targets, so you learn how to shoot at different angles.

Most hunters tend to shoot behind crossing targets and below those that are rising, especially at long ranges. If you miss consistently, double your lead after each shot until you hit your mark.

PULL the trigger when you think you have reached the proper lead. Do not hesitate, flinch or slow down your swing as you pull the trigger.

FOLLOW THROUGH until the barrel is well past the bird. If you stop swinging too soon, you will shoot behind the target.

How to Estimate Shooting Range

COMPARE the head-to-tail length of a crossing bird to the muzzle width of your shotgun. At 20 yards (left), a mallard duck appears nearly twice as long as the width of a 12 gauge shotgun's muzzle. At 45 yards (right), the

bird's length is about the same as the width of the muzzle. A large Canada goose is almost twice as long as the muzzle at 30 yards; slightly longer at 45 yards; and approximately the same length at 60 yards.

Bowhunting

Bowhunters face the ultimate hunting challenge. A bow lacks the accuracy and range of a modern firearm, so you must fine-tune your skills to get close enough for an effective shot.

Yet bowhunting is rapidly gaining popularity. Most states and provinces consider the bow and arrow a primitive weapon. They allow bowhunters to take big game weeks before the regular firearms season. Many states also conduct post-season bow hunts.

Another reason for the expanding interest in bowhunting is the *compound bow*. Cams and pulleys on the compound produce more energy than a conventional bow with the same *draw weight*, or the pounds of pull required to bring a 28-inch arrow to full draw. On some compound bows, hunters can substitute special elliptical cams to increase energy even more.

Cams also result in *let-off*. At full draw, you must hold only one-half to two-thirds of the bow's draw weight. This enables you to use a more powerful bow. It also reduces muscle fatigue, so you can hold steady at full draw while awaiting the opportune moment for a shot.

Some hunters still prefer *recurve* and *long* bows. They are lighter, quieter to shoot, and less prone to

Equipment for Bowhunting

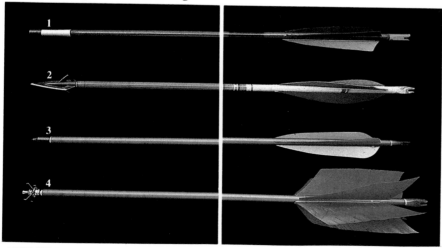

ARROWHEADS include: (1) blunts for small game, (2) broadheads with razor inserts for big game, (3) target points, (4) Judos® for birds and small game. Fletchings include: (1) and (2) feather, which provides the most stable flight; (3) plastic, which is waterproof and durable; (4) flu-flu, which slows the arrow.

BOW QUIVERS hold the arrows so they do not rattle. A plastic cover protects the points. You can remove an arrow quickly and with little motion.

mechanical failure. These more traditional bows increase the challenge and add nostalgia to the hunt.

For deer hunting, choose a bow with a draw weight of at least 40 pounds. For elk, you need a draw weight of 50 pounds or more. Do not select a bow with a draw weight heavier than you can comfortably handle.

Always match your arrows to your bow. When choosing arrows, consider stiffness, or *spine*. The more powerful the bow, the stiffer the arrow. The spine of your arrow should be rated within 5 pounds of your bow's draw weight.

Arrow weight is also important. A heavy arrow penetrates better, but drops more than a light one. Check an arrow chart at an archery shop to help you select the heaviest shaft that still matches your bow.

Most bowhunters use aluminum, fiberglass, and fiberglass-graphite arrows. These shafts come in a wide variety of weights and stiffnesses, and they never warp. Some hunters still use wood shafts. They are inexpensive, but sometimes vary in weight and stiffness, and may warp. Unmatched or warped shafts cannot be shot with consistent accuracy. Of all the materials, aluminum offers the greatest consistency because the shafts can be closely matched in weight and spine.

Before buying arrows, measure your *draw length.* This is the distance from the string to the *back,* or far side of the bow, as you hold at full draw. The arrow should extend just beyond the back of the bow.

Many arrow shafts come with a threaded coupling on the end, enabling you to switch points for target shooting or hunting.

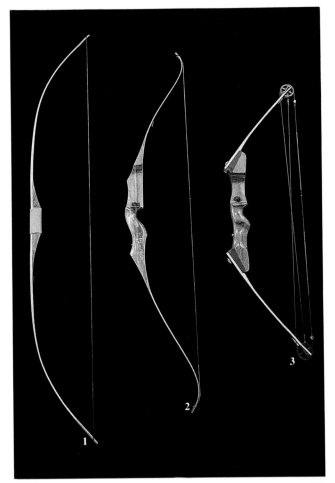

BOWS include: (1) long bows, (2) recurve bows, (3) compound bows. Compounds deliver the most energy for a given draw weight; long bows the least. A compound's limbs are fiberglass or fiberglass-wood laminates. Long bows and recurves are usually made of fiberglass-wood laminates, though some long bows are solid wood.

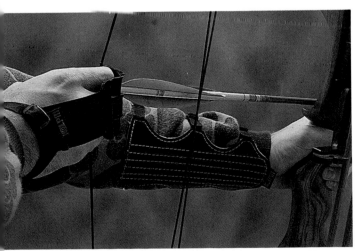

GUARDS for arms and fingers protect your skin and improve accuracy. Finger guards help you release the bowstring smoothly. Arm guards prevent the bowstring from catching your sleeve or slapping against your arm.

ACCESSORY KITS attach to a belt. They can hold extra bowstrings; bowstring wax, which preserves the string and keeps it dry; bottled scents to mask human odor; camouflage makeup; and interchangeable arrowheads.

Shooting a Bow and Arrow

In the hands of an expert, the bow and arrow is surprisingly accurate. But the average hunter stands little chance of killing an animal with a bow, unless he is willing to take time to practice.

Shooting a bow and arrow accurately is more difficult than shooting a firearm. You must build up your arm, shoulder and back muscles in order to hold steady at full draw. And because an arrow drops much more than a bullet, you must develop a feel for shooting at different distances.

Accurate shooting requires a consistent draw and release. To develop consistency, practice in your back yard or at an archery range. Be sure to use a

nocking point, a small metal ring that attaches to your bowstring. The *nock,* or notched end of the arrow, rests just under the ring, so each arrow releases from the same point on the string.

Many archers use bow sights, which usually have several *sight pins,* each set to compensate for arrow drop at different distances. To adjust bow sights, simply move the pin in the direction of your error. For example, if the arrow hits too far to the right, move the sight pin to the right. If the arrow hits low, move the sight pin down.

To shoot accurately with sights, you must be a good judge of distance. Sights are not practical for running or flying animals. Under these conditions, you can shoot better by instinct. Shooting a bow and arrow instinctively is much like throwing a ball. Let

How to Shoot a Bow and Arrow

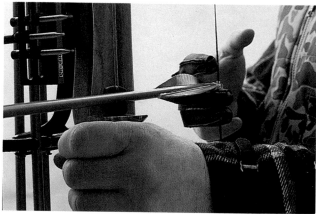

NOCK the arrow below the nocking point; lay the shaft across the arrow rest. Curl your fingers around the bowstring. Your index finger should be above the arrow, with your middle and ring fingers below. Keep the back of your hand straight.

STAND crossways to the target with your feet shoulder-width apart. If you are right-handed, your right foot should be even with or slightly ahead of your left. Lean slightly forward with the upper half of your body, so most of your weight is on your left foot.

How Different Bows Affect Your Shooting

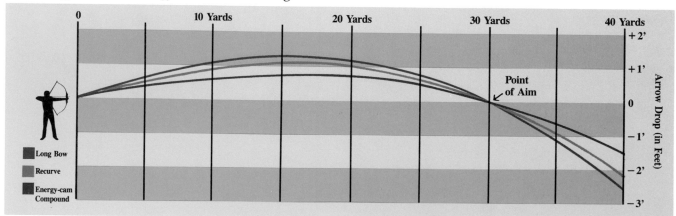

PERFORMANCE of arrows depends on the type of bow. Identical 550-grain arrows were shot from a long bow, a recurve, and an energy-cam compound, each with a draw weight of 60 pounds. The chart shows that compound bows have the flattest trajectory, followed by re-

curve and long bows. When tested at 20 yards, the arrow from the long bow had a velocity of 155 feet-per-second and struck with 29 foot-pounds of energy; from the recurve, 166 fps and 34 ft. lbs.; from the compound, 199 fps and 48 ft. lbs.

your senses tell you how high to aim at various distances. Many good bowhunters use this technique, especially for moving targets.

Always practice from the positions in which you hunt. If you use a tree stand, practice from an elevated platform. If you sit in your stand, practice in the sitting position. Wear your hunting clothes because they may affect your shooting. When you can routinely place your arrows in a plate-sized circle at 30 yards, you are ready to go hunting.

If you cannot shoot consistently, you are probably making one of the following mistakes:
• The bow may be too powerful, causing you to shake when you release the arrow.
• Too little spine causes an arrow to veer right if you shoot right-handed; too much causes it to veer left.

• The nocking point may be in the wrong position, causing your arrows to fly erratically.
• You may be *pulling off,* or pulling your hand away from your face on the release.
• You may be overdrawing or underdrawing the bow, causing your arrows to hit high or low.

Responsible hunters seldom take shots over 40 yards because of the risk of hitting an animal outside the vital area. Most shots are from 10 to 20 yards.

Some bowhunters can hit walking animals or even flying birds. But a standing shot offers the best chance for a kill. To assure a standing shot once you spot an animal, you must be well camouflaged and stay nearly motionless. Wait until the animal looks away before drawing the bow. It will be less likely to detect your movement and bolt before you shoot.

DRAW the string to your *anchor point.* Most shooters place the forefinger at the corner of the mouth. Use the same anchor point each time and hold the bow steady.

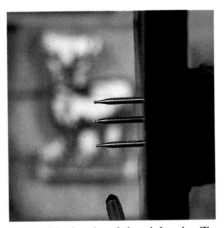

AIM with the tip of the sight pin. To hit this target (30 yards), hold the 30-yard pin (red tip) on the vital area. Hold the pin slightly lower at 25 yards; slightly higher at 35 yards.

RELEASE the string by quickly relaxing your fingers, so the string slips free. Hold the bow steady until the arrow strikes. If you move the bow too soon, the arrow will fly erratically.

Tips for Shooting a Bow and Arrow

BUILD a practice target from excelsior or hay bales. Stack three bales on a pair of 2 × 8 planks. Lay two, 2 × 6s across the top and string fence wire through the boards. On each side, insert a rod through a loop in the wire, then turn the rod to tighten the wire.

PACE off different yardages in the area surrounding your stand. This enables you to gauge shooting distance accurately, so you can properly line up your bow sights. Some bowhunters make cuts in dead branches or logs to identify 10-yard intervals.

BURNING POWDER causes a fiery explosion when you shoot a muzzleloader. The cloud of smoke may obscure your target. Some hunters wear frontier costumes to recreate the mood of a primitive hunt.

Muzzleloaders

The allure of a muzzleloader involves a combination of greater challenge, increased hunting opportunity, and the nostalgia of using a primitive weapon.

Muzzleloaders, or black powder weapons, must be loaded by inserting the powder, and bullet or shot into the muzzle. The most popular types for hunting include rifles, smoothbore muskets, and shotguns.

The bullets used in muzzleloading rifles are generally large caliber, varying from round lead balls to blunt-nosed cylinders, called *Maxi-Balls*. Slow-burning black powder does not have the explosive power of modern, smokeless powder. This limits the killing range to about 80 to 120 yards, depending on the bullet and the powder charge.

Muzzleloader bullets lack the velocity of modern rifle bullets, so their trajectories are not as flat. They do not mushroom like rifle bullets, but they flatten on impact to deliver extra shocking power.

The challenge of shooting a black-powder rifle results from its limited range and long reloading time, about one minute per barrel. Because of these limitations, many states offer more liberal regulations to muzzleloader hunters. Some hold special seasons before or after the regular firearms season.

Black powder shotguns and muskets have not gained the popularity of muzzleloading rifles. But black powder shotguns work surprisingly well for birds and small game. Muskets lack the accuracy of rifles, because the bores do not have rifling grooves.

Most black powder enthusiasts use factory-made replicas of the original guns or make their own from kits. A few hunters use the originals. But discharging an old gun can be dangerous and may reduce its value. Have a gunsmith inspect it first.

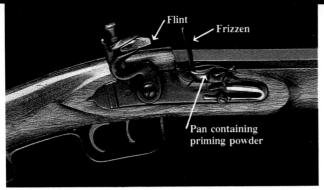

Flint
Frizzen
Pan containing
priming powder

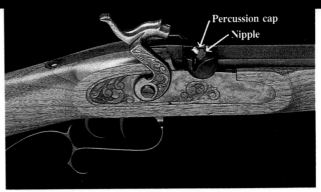

Percussion cap
Nipple

FLINTLOCKS have a flint in the hammer. When the flint strikes a frizzen, sparks ignite the primer powder. Flame passes through a vent to set off the powder charge. The exposed firing mechanism may fail in damp weather.

CAPLOCKS are more reliable than flintlocks. The hammer strikes a percussion cap, similar to the primer of a modern cartridge. A flash travels through the nipple to ignite the powder charge.

How to Load a Muzzleloader

POUR the powder down the muzzle directly from a measuring device. Never pour black powder from an open flask. It may ignite, causing the flask to explode.

SEAT a round ball on a lubricated patch; grease the grooves of a Maxi-Ball. Start either with the stubby end of a *short starter*. Place the long end on the ball, then strike starter firmly.

PUSH the ball the rest of the way down the barrel with a *ramrod*. Keep pushing until the ball is seated firmly against the powder charge. Never use the ramrod to start the ball.

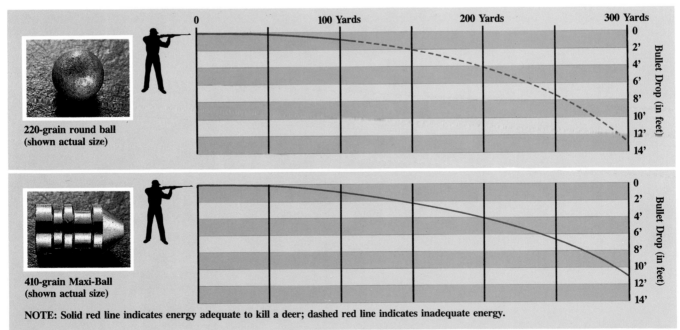

220-grain round ball (shown actual size)

410-grain Maxi-Ball (shown actual size)

NOTE: Solid red line indicates energy adequate to kill a deer; dashed red line indicates inadequate energy.

PERFORMANCE of muzzleloader bullets differs greatly. A .54 caliber, 220-grain muzzleloader round ball drops 8.9 inches at 100 yards and has enough energy to kill a deer out to 110 yards. A .54 caliber, 410-grain Maxi-Ball drops 10.7 inches at 100 yards, but retains enough energy to kill a deer beyond 300 yards. However, at 300 yards, the Maxi-Ball has dropped about 132 inches, making an accurate shot almost impossible.

45

Hunting Safety

Most people would be surprised to learn that hunting is not among the most dangerous sports. A National Safety Council study showed the fatality rate for hunting to be less than half that of boating or swimming.

Improved hunter education and increased use of fluorescent orange clothing account for the low accident rate. Every state and province sponsors some type of firearms safety or hunter education program. Many states require beginning hunters to pass such a course before they can purchase a license.

Nevertheless, the potential for a serious accident always exists. To avoid an accident, follow these safety rules.

- Treat every firearm as if it is loaded. Never assume a gun is unloaded because someone said so.

- Never point a weapon at anything you do not mean to shoot. This includes glassing other hunters with your rifle scope.

KEEP the safety on and your finger away from the trigger until you are ready to shoot. This eliminates the possibility of discharging the gun accidentally, especially if you stumble or fall.

Planning Firing Zones

ESTABLISH safe firing zones when hunting with others. When driving game, hunters should shoot only within the zones indicated by arrows.

POSITION your boat sideways to the shooting area. Do not position the boat lengthwise; this places one hunter in the other's shooting zone.

SPLIT the area around your blind into 180-degree shooting zones. Each hunter scans for birds in the semicircle around his half of the blind.

- Make sure your safety is on at all times, unless you intend to shoot.

- Positively identify your target before shooting. Never fire at a silhouette, a vague form, or an area where you saw or heard something move. Fluorescent orange clothing will greatly improve your own visibility.

- Control the direction of your muzzle at all times. If you start to fall, point the barrel away from yourself and other hunters. After a fall, check the barrel for obstructions like dirt or snow. A plugged barrel could rupture when you shoot, possibly causing serious injury.

- Never lean a gun against a tree, fencepost, vehicle or any place where it could fall over and accidentally discharge.

- Never shoot at hard surfaces or water with bullets or slugs. They could ricochet and strike another hunter or a building.

- Never drink alcoholic beverages before or during a hunt. Alcohol will not keep you warm; instead, it speeds the loss of body heat.

- Use only the ammunition recommended for your firearm. Do not carry two different types of ammunition in your pocket at the same time.

- When not hunting, keep the gun unloaded and the action open.

- Keep all firearms and ammunition out of the reach of children.

- Refuse to hunt with anyone who does not observe the basic rules of firearms safety.

NEVER SHOOT unless you can see your target clearly. In dim light (above) you may see a form that resembles a game animal. The bottom photo reveals that the form is actually that of a hunter.

Other Safety Tips

NEVER SHOOT if there is a chance of hitting buildings, livestock, or any other unintended target. Avoid shooting over the tops of hills and ridges.

OPEN your action before crossing a creek, climbing over a fence, or in any other situation where you are unsure of your footing.

CARRY your firearm so the muzzle points away from others. Safe positions (left to right) include: shoulder carry, cradle carry, and trail carry.

47

Hunting Strategies

Planning Your Hunt

ALWAYS ASK for permission to hunt on private land. Introduce yourself and specify the type of game you wish to hunt. Some landowners will grant permission to a courteous hunter, even though their land is posted.

Advance planning is the key to a good hunting trip. Whether you travel to another state or hunt around home, lay the groundwork for your trip early.

Preparations for an out-of-state hunt should begin a year ahead. Some states conduct drawings for non-resident permits to hunt animals like elk, deer, pronghorn or wild turkey. Most states accept applications until spring, but some set deadlines as early as mid-winter.

Begin planning your trip by requesting non-resident hunting information from the wildlife agency in the state or province where you plan to hunt. Be sure to specify the type of game you will be hunting. Ask about drawing application deadlines and information on state and federal wildlife areas that may require advance reservations. Licenses may be offered on a first-come, first-served basis. Some states require hunters to show evidence of having passed a firearms safety or hunter education course.

Reservations and permits may also be necessary when hunting in your own state. Wildlife managers and conservation officers can provide information on special hunts that require advance preparation. They can also supply current game census data to help you choose a hunting area. Managers may know of local farmers or ranchers who want hunters to thin over-abundant game populations.

Many hunters join sportsmen's clubs, where they can share information on local game populations and habitat conditions. Some clubs lease private land where members can hunt.

Late summer is the best time to contact private landowners. Some farmers and ranchers tire of frequent interruptions during the hunting season. Once you get to know a landowner, you can phone ahead for permission to hunt rather than disturb him in early morning or interrupt his work.

TALK to a clerk at a sporting goods store for local hunting information. Many stores employ knowledgeable hunters. Most carry maps, permit applications and other items for planning your hunt.

GATHER information from state and federal wildlife agencies. They supply maps, brochures on public hunting areas, public access lists, and regulations. Tourist bureaus can recommend motels, resorts and campgrounds.

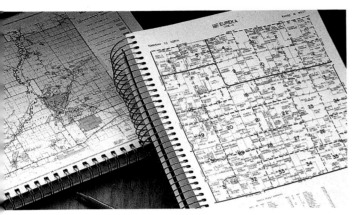

COUNTY MAPS (left) identify paved and unpaved roads. They also show section lines, buildings, public lands, lakes and streams. Plat books (right) detail property lines and identify landowners. The maps and plat books are usually available at county offices.

AERIAL PHOTOGRAPHS reveal important details lacking on maps. They show isolated ponds and marshes, small streams, vegetation types, logging areas, meadows and forest trails. They can be obtained from the U.S. Department of Agriculture and private survey firms.

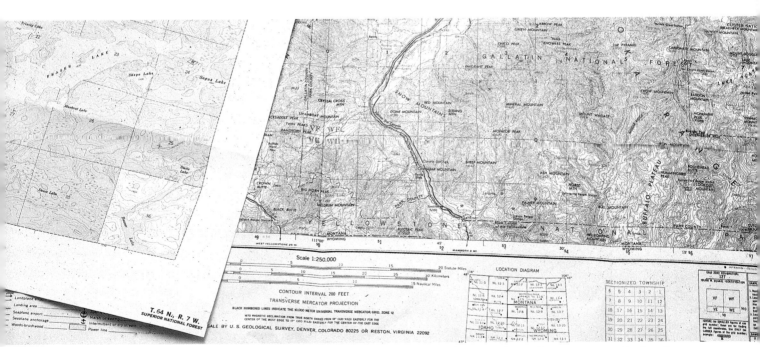

TOPOGRAPHIC MAPS, like the U.S. Forest Service map (left) and the U.S. Geological Survey map (right), provide information on land elevation and detail other features of the landscape, such as wetlands. They also show buildings, roads, trails, portages and other features useful for finding your way on a hunting trip. Geological Survey maps show forested areas in green. They generally cover a larger area than Forest Service maps.

51

Scouting for Game

Pre-season scouting will improve your odds of finding game once the hunting season begins. Scouting is enjoyable in itself and saves valuable hunting time later.

Scouting enables you to become familiar with the terrain and to identify heavily-used game trails. It also helps you to determine any changes in habitat conditions or fluctuations in game populations that could affect your hunting.

Severe winter storms, wildlife food shortages, drought, and cold or wet weather during nesting can drastically reduce game populations. New roads, housing developments and wetland drainage can permanently eliminate good wildlife habitat. So, there is no guarantee that last year's prime hunting spot will produce game this year.

Binoculars and spotting scopes will help you find game from a distant vantage point. But even if you do not see animals, you can detect their presence by the signs they leave. Squirrels build nests in trees and scatter nut shells on the ground. Waterfowl preen themselves and leave feathers around resting areas. Bull elk bugle and roll in wallows during the mating period. All animals can be identified from their tracks and droppings.

GLASS a potential hunting area from a nearby hill or tree. Look closely at edges between openings and cover to detect movement. You are most likely to see game early in the morning, at dusk or on cloudy days. When you spot an animal, note the time and identify a landmark to pinpoint the exact location. If the animal is not disturbed, it may appear in the same area at about the same time on subsequent days.

TRACKS in damp soil may reveal how long ago an animal passed. Fresh tracks (left) have sharp edges. Older tracks (right) have fuzzy edges. In snow, old tracks have a hard crust.

DROPPINGS help hunters find game. Large quantities indicate feeding, loafing or bedding areas. Some animals do not digest their food completely, so you can check droppings to determine what they have been eating.

FEEDING SIGNS include damaged crops; scratched earth; nipped ends on grasses or twigs; and pits, husks and shells of fruits or nuts. Experienced hunters can often identify an animal by these signs.

DAMAGED TREES AND BRUSH result from animals rubbing velvet from their antlers, scratching trees to mark their territory, or chewing bark. Each species has distinctive rubs, scrapes and chews.

BEDS AND ROOSTS in tall grass or on soft earth reveal the resting spots of mammals and birds. You can identify the animal from the size of its bed or roost and from nearby droppings, hair or feathers.

GAME TRAILS lead from cover to food or water. Several kinds of game often use the same trail. Inspect it closely and look for fresh tracks made by the animals you will be hunting.

Still-hunting

WALK slowly and quietly. Avoid turning your head quickly, swinging your arms, or making other movements that animals associate with humans.

A still-hunter must pit his senses against those of his quarry. The term *still,* used this way, means silent, not motionless.

When still-hunting, always move slowly, keeping alert for sounds, visual signs and even odors that reveal the presence of game. When you move slowly, it is easier to see and hear animals, but more difficult for them to detect you.

Still-hunting works best when game is not active. Many hunters prefer to stand-hunt (page 56) in early morning, still-hunt during midday, then return to their stands in late afternoon.

The typical strategy is to walk at an extremely slow pace, taking only a few steps at a time. Stop, then wait for at least as long as you walked, slowly moving only your head and eyes. The length of each walking and waiting period varies, depending on the type of animal you are hunting. The periods are generally short for small game, but up to five minutes or longer for big game.

Whenever possible, walk into the wind so animals cannot detect your scent. Place each footstep carefully to prevent snapping twigs, crunching leaves or brushing against branches. Avoid crossing open areas and places where animals could see your form above the horizon. Try to stay near cover where game will not notice your movements.

The still-hunter does not know the exact location of an animal. Instead, he moves through likely-looking cover in hopes of surprising game. Expert hunters may get so close that animals burst from cover near their feet.

Still-hunting is usually a one-hunter method, but it also works well with two. Game surprised by one person may run toward the other. Or an animal may be so intent on watching one hunter that it does not detect another approaching.

Successful still-hunting demands patience and confidence. If you lose patience and begin moving too fast, animals will spook. If you are confident of seeing game, it is easier to stay alert.

Tips for Still-hunting

WEAR soft clothing to reduce noise. Hard-finish materials like nylon make swishing sounds as they brush the cover. Gummy bootsoles enable you to walk quietly.

TEST the direction of subtle wind currents by tossing a small amount of down into the air. Many hunters keep a small bag of down in their pocket.

LOOK for visual clues to find game. A horizontal line among trees could be an animal's back. A glinting eye or twitching ear could also reveal game.

AVOID walking or waiting in direct sunlight. Animals are quick to notice the glare off your face and clothing. They are less likely to see a hunter in the shade.

PORTABLE STANDS enable you to change location quickly. This tree stand clamps to the trunk in seconds. It has a comfortable seat and, when placed well above ground level, offers a wide field of vision. An elevated stand keeps your scent above the ground and places you higher than the usual sight plane of game.

Stand-hunting

The secret to successful stand-hunting is to position yourself where you are likely to see game, but game is not likely to see you. The technique works best early or late in the day, when animals move between resting and feeding areas.

Hunters conceal themselves on *stands* or in *blinds*. A stand may be nothing more than a large tree that obscures your form. Or it may be an elevated platform, either free-standing or attached to a tree trunk or limb. A blind provides more cover. Many have walls of camouflage material or vegetation.

Whether hunting from a blind or stand, choose a spot where game is likely to pass. Scout the area to find heavily-used game trails or flight paths. Take your position and get ready well before game begins moving. You may have to find your spot in the dark.

The wind can play a major role in choosing your site. When hunting big game, take a stand down-wind of the area where you expect to see animals. Select alternative locations for different wind conditions. To insure that animals will not detect human scent, many hunters mask their odor with bottled scents from skunks or other animals. Never smoke while stand-hunting. The sight and smell of smoke will alert game.

Wind direction is also important when hunting ducks or geese on water. Choose a blind on the lee side of natural cover. Waterfowl usually land into the wind in the calmer water.

Stand-hunters sometimes wear camouflage outfits to reduce their visibility. But many types of hunting require high-visibility clothing for safety purposes. Even if you wear fluorescent orange clothing, game will be less likely to see you if you keep motion to a minimum. If you must move, do so very slowly. Keep your face hidden; look at game from the side of your eye or from behind a hat brim.

Comfort is important when stand-hunting. You cannot remain quiet and motionless if you are cold, wet or in an uncomfortable position. You need warm clothing, because you must remain stationary for long periods. Some hunters build roofs to shed rain, or use padded seats and stoves. Waterfowl hunters sometimes build blinds that are completely enclosed except for shooting windows.

LOCATE your stand or blind near a watering site or stream crossing. Dove and antelope hunters often hunt near water holes. Moose hunters carefully check streambanks for heavily-used trails leading to water.

CHOOSE a site near a feeding area. Goose hunters build blinds or dig pits in harvested fields. Deer hunters take stands along the edges of corn, hay or milo fields. Bear hunters sometimes bait an area, then hunt nearby.

SELECT a spot that offers a good view of the area where you expect game to appear. Many hunters prefer stands that overlook clearings. Some cut their own shooting lanes in timber or bush.

AVOID stands that do not offer a clear field of fire. A tree or branch too close to your stand will narrow your shooting zone. A stand that restricts hip movement makes it difficult to swing your gun.

Stalking

Like still-hunting, stalking demands fine-tuned hunting skills, because you must slip up on game without being detected. Stalking differs from still-hunting in that you know the location of the animal. Sneaking within shooting range can be extremely difficult, but expert stalkers often approach within a few feet of game.

Many stalkers use binoculars or spotting scopes. Because you can see an animal from farther away, it is less likely to detect you before you can adequately plan your strategy. When you spot an animal, watch it closely for a few minutes to determine whether it is likely to remain in the same area long enough for a stalk. If the animal is moving or appears nervous, you will probably not be able to get close enough for a shot. If it is feeding or bedded down, your odds are much better.

Stalking works best where the topography or cover will conceal your approach. Before beginning your stalk, plot a course that takes you into the wind, but keeps you behind hills, trees, fencelines, or other natural or man-made features.

If there is no cover, use a clump of vegetation to break up your outline. Camouflage clothing will also make you less visible. Move only when the animal faces away from you or when its head is down. Be sure that sunlight does not reflect off your gun or scope. If the animal sees you, walk away until you are out of sight. It may resume what it was doing, giving you another opportunity.

Move silently during the final stages of the stalk. Noise may not be important if you shoot from 300 yards. But for the bowhunter who must approach within 30 yards, any noise can ruin his chances.

It is usually best to stay concealed until after the shot. But waterfowl hunters sometimes rush the birds before they shoot. They may gain an extra 5 to 10 yards before the birds take off.

How to Stalk Game

PINPOINT game by identifying nearby landmarks like a tree, boulder or fencepost. You can stay hidden, while using the landmark to guide your approach.

PLAN your stalk so you move directly into or quarter into the wind. This prevents the wind from carrying your scent and the sound of your approach to the animal.

USE natural cover to conceal your approach. A fence-line, a drainage ditch, or a field of tall crops or grass will enable you to sneak within gun range.

BRING your own cover when hunting in flat, open country. Push a clump of weeds ahead of you, and stay low so game cannot spot your form above the horizon.

Driving

A lone hunter has little chance of rousting game from a large expanse of cover. Most animals sit tight or move off to the side rather than run or fly.

Driving is an effective way to push game out of cover. You can make a drive with as few as two or over a dozen hunters, depending on the situation. Before the drive begins, *posters* sneak to positions at the end of cover, where they intercept game pushed to them by *drivers*. The drivers spread out across the field or woods. The denser the vegetation, the closer they must be to discourage game from doubling back between them. It is generally better to have more drivers than posters.

Drives work best in a corridor or block of cover surrounded by open land. Game will usually stay in the cover until pushed to the end, assuring someone of a shot. If possible, start at the widest end and work toward the narrowest. This concentrates the animals in a relatively small area, increasing your chances of a close shot.

Hunters should always know the position of other drivers and posters. Wear fluorescent orange clothing for maximum visibility and never shoot in the direction of another hunter.

DRIVERS should stay within sight of each other. Outside drivers often move ahead to prevent game from escaping out the sides. Be especially alert as drivers approach posters; cornered game may spring from cover.

Where to Conduct a Drive

ISLANDS of cover are ideal for drives. A patch of high brush in an open field, a shelterbelt or a woodlot is likely to hold game. If you attempt to hunt these areas alone, game may escape out the opposite side.

CORRIDORS of cover, like roadside ditches, canyons, stream courses and railroad tracks, make good places for a drive. Game is less likely to double back in a narrow strip of cover than in a wide expanse.

Flushing

For many types of game, the surest way to evade hunters is to hide in dense cover. Even animals as large as a deer or as brightly colored as a rooster pheasant can hide within a few feet of hunters without being noticed.

Hunters who use dogs stand the best chance of flushing tight-holding animals. Even in thick brush or other dense cover, a good dog will detect and follow an animal's scent. Without a dog, you are sure to walk by some game.

A lone hunter can unnerve animals, causing them to flush. Unusual sounds and erratic movements may cause game to become nervous and burst from cover. Many hunters yell, clap their hands, crack brush or even blow whistles as they walk. By varying your walking speed, stopping, turning back suddenly, or even running a few steps, you may convince an animal that it has been discovered.

When hunting with a partner, try to flush game toward each other. Start at opposite ends of the cover and attempt to trap game in the middle. This cuts off possible escape routes. And because the animal detects danger from two directions, it is more likely to flush.

STOP frequently when attempting to flush game. If you walk at a steady pace, animals usually sit tight because they are confident they have not been detected. When you stop, they lose confidence and attempt to escape.

Tips for Flushing Game

THROW sticks or rocks to flush game from dense brush piles or other cover too thick to walk through. Game will usually attempt to slip out the opposite side, so watch carefully and be ready for a shot.

KICK or step on clumps of vegetation that could hold birds or small game. With a hunter this close, game may be reluctant to flush. Tracks, droppings, feathers or hair may reveal the animal's presence.

RETRIEVERS include the Labrador retriever (above), golden retriever, Chesapeake Bay retriever and American water spaniel. These breeds are well-suited for retrieving waterfowl, because their skin secretes an oily substance that sheds water. Most retrievers also flush and retrieve upland game birds.

Hunting Dogs

One of the hunter's most valuable assets is a well-trained hunting dog. Watching a good dog in action adds to the thrill of the hunt. And a dog with flushing, pointing or retrieving skills will greatly improve your hunting success.

Before selecting a dog, consider the type of game you intend to hunt, the terrain and climate. Pointing and flushing breeds were originally developed for hunting upland birds, most retrievers for waterfowl, and most hounds for small game. Many breeds work well for more than one type of game. The Labrador, for example, is an excellent waterfowl retriever, but is also favored by many upland bird hunters for its flushing skills.

When hunting upland birds in a large expanse of light cover, use a dog that ranges widely. Pointing breeds work beyond gun range. When they detect a strong scent, they freeze in position, or *point*. This gives the hunter time to walk in and flush the bird. For finding birds in thicker cover, a flushing dog may work better. These dogs work the cover slowly and thoroughly, usually staying within gun range.

Thorny cover can penetrate the fur and cut a short-haired dog. Long-haired breeds can tolerate thorns, but their fur often becomes matted with burrs.

In cold weather, a heavy-coated breed retains body heat longer than a dog with a thin coat. A thick coat is especially important for a dog that must retrieve in icy water. In extremely hot weather, a thin-coated breed works best. A dog with thick fur would overheat quickly.

A hunter must learn to *read* his dog, because every dog behaves somewhat differently when it smells game. With a pointing dog, a loose point usually means that the game has slipped away. A staunch point generally means game is close. Retrieving and flushing breeds perk up their ears or wag their tails rapidly. Hounds bay when they detect game.

Proper training and conditioning are the keys to developing a good dog. A poorly-trained dog is worse than no dog at all. If it does not obey basic commands, it may flush game out of range. Or the dog may run off, costing you hours of hunting time.

Pre-season conditioning helps a dog maintain its stamina and toughens its feet. Run your dog at least one-half hour several times a week during summer.

POINTING BREEDS include the English Pointer (above), German shorthair, Brittany spaniel, English setter, Gordon setter and weimaraner. These breeds are used mainly for upland birds, but a few hunters use them for rabbits and squirrels. Many pointers will also retrieve downed game.

FLUSHERS include several types of spaniels, like the springer (above), cocker and Boykin. These breeds pursue game until it flushes from cover, so they should be trained to work within gun range. The springer is especially popular among pheasant hunters.

HOUNDS, like the black-and-tan (left) and redtick (right), have highly sensitive noses and are used mainly for trailing small game. Some, like the beagle, also work well for game birds. Other hounds include the bluetick, Walker and redbone.

Float-hunting

Water offers hunters an excellent means for approaching game silently. And a float-hunter can cover a large area with relatively little effort.

Float-hunting works best for waterfowl, squirrels, deer, moose and other animals that frequent streambanks and lakeshores. You can also float up on flocks, or *rafts,* of waterfowl in open water.

Most float-hunters use small, low-profile watercraft including jon boats, canoes, semi-Vs and sculling boats. Boats are usually painted camouflage colors or draped with natural vegetation, netting or camouflage cloth.

The best boat depends on the area you hunt and the type of hunting. A jon boat is very stable, but the square bow would not slide through dense cattails. A canoe or double-pointed duck boat is less stable, but would slip through easily. A deep semi-V is best for rough water, but because of its high profile would not be a good choice for floating up on waterfowl. The birds would be less likely to notice a shallow-draft, sculling boat.

Silence is the key to float-hunting success. You can paddle very quietly in a canoe. If you row a boat, make sure the oars do not squeak or scrape the gunwales. Keep loose items tied down and try not to move around in the boat. Wood and fiberglass hulls are quieter than aluminum hulls. Many hunters glue carpet or rubber matting to the bottom, seats and gunwales to muffle sounds.

Keep safety in mind when float-hunting. Wear a life preserver or sit on a buoyant cushion. Never hunt from a tippy boat. It may flip over if you stand up to shoot or when your dog plunges into the water to retrieve game. To stabilize a canoe or other small watercraft, add *sponsons,* or bands of buoyant material, to the side of the hull. Low-profile boats make you less visible, but they can be dangerous on large, wind-swept waters.

How to Float-hunt a Stream

FLOAT from one point to the next (dotted line). The points will conceal your approach, enabling you to slip up on game downstream. Your boat would be visible from farther away if you followed the outside bends.

DRIFT stern-first in fast water. The oarsman sits in the bow and rows quietly to slow the boat's drift. The shooter sits in the stern, where he has a clear field of fire without shooting over the oarsman.

How to Pole Through Heavy Cover

POLE through cane, cattails, bulrushes or other high vegetation to jump waterfowl and other game. Some hunters use push-poles as long as 16 feet to propel narrow watercraft through the weeds.

USE a duck-bill on your push-pole. When you push, the bill spreads, preventing the pole from sinking deep into the mud and causing you to lose leverage. When you pull, the bill closes so it slides easily out of the mud.

How to Use a Sculling Boat

MANEUVER a sculling boat with a specially designed oar that fits through a hole in the transom. To propel the boat, move the curved blade back and forth in a figure-eight fashion.

LIE DOWN in the boat so you can float up on game without being detected. Start upwind and let the wind push you within shooting range. Most hunters paint their sculling boats gray to blend in with the water.

BLOOD TRAILS may provide clues for pursuing wounded game. Bright red, frothy blood indicates a lung shot and tells you to follow immediately. Darker blood usually means a less damaging hit; wait before following.

How to Find Downed Game

Losing a wounded animal is one of the greatest frustrations in hunting. Finding downed game requires patience and persistence. But conscientious hunters make every effort to recover game that has been hit.

After the shot, watch the animal closely and try to determine if you made a clean kill, wounded it or missed completely. Clean kills and misses are usually obvious, but it may be more difficult to recognize a wounded animal. Even if you see no sign of a hit, look for hair or feathers, erratic movement or unusual behavior. You might hear the impact when your bullet strikes a big game animal.

Dogs with good retrieving skills greatly improve your chances of finding downed birds and small game. A dog will mark a bird down and promptly retrieve it. If it runs, the dog will circle to pick up the scent, then follow the scent trail.

Follow up any shot at big game, because large animals may show little evidence of being hit. Despite its size, a wounded deer can be as difficult to find as a cottontail. Unless hit in a vital area, it may run a long distance, especially if pursued by hunters.

If you are sure you hit a vital area, begin your pursuit immediately. An animal shot in the heart-lung area will seldom run farther than 100 yards. If you suspect a less damaging hit, it may be better to wait before following. A bleeding animal may lie down if not pursued. After 30 to 60 minutes, it will probably be too weak to run. Do not wait to follow if rain or snow threatens to obscure the blood trail.

Basics of Finding Downed Game

MARK the spot where you last saw the animal. Look for an obvious landmark, like a tree, or leave a piece of clothing at the spot. Work outward in widening circles, but return if you fail to find the animal.

LOOK for feathers, hair or blood where you suspect the animal to be. Stand still, listen for movement, then inspect nearby cover. Hunters may fail to find game by leaving too soon, thinking the animal has run off.

How to Find Wounded Big Game

MOVE QUIETLY and watch ahead for movement when trailing big game. If you fail to see the animal and approach too closely, you may frighten it off, making it more difficult to find. Locating downed game is easiest with two or more hunters. While one inspects the ground for blood, the other looks for any signs of movement. If you lose the trail, mark the spot where you last saw blood. Then you can resume the search at that point.

How to Find Downed Birds and Small Game

CHECK likely escape routes if you cannot find the animal. Wounded game may slip into a strip of grass connected to the main cover area.

EXAMINE thick clumps of grass or brush patches for signs of the animal. A protruding tail reveals the location of this wounded pheasant.

WORK your dog just downwind of downed game. If the dog does not pick up the scent, call it to the spot where you last saw the animal.

Hunting Wild Game

Hunting Big Game

Few sports are as challenging, demanding or rewarding as big game hunting. Hunters must match wits with animals perfectly adapted to their environment. They often have to walk miles over rugged terrain or carry out carcasses that exceed 1000 pounds. But the rewards are great: a sense of accomplishment, a memorable trophy and a supply of prime-quality meat.

Big game hunting success depends on an understanding of your quarry. For example, during the rut, many big game animals lose their normal caution and spend more time away from cover. If you plan your hunt during this brief period, you can greatly improve your chances of bagging a trophy.

Scouting is especially important when hunting big game, because an animal's daily movement is predictable. If you find a fresh trail, a bedding area or feeding site, chances are that game will frequent these spots on subsequent days.

Big game hunters should know how to use a compass and survival gear. If you hunt in a forest or in the mountains, you could easily become disoriented. Study aerial photos or maps before you hunt a new area and carry them while hunting. By identifying prominent landmarks, you can avoid getting

lost. Maps and photos also help you find good hunting spots.

Proper physical conditioning can make hunting more enjoyable, especially if you hunt in steep or mountainous terrain. If you are out of condition or have blisters on your feet, it can be a chore to walk up a hill with a rifle and backpack, let alone drag out a large animal. To get themselves in shape, many hunters jog several times a week during summer. Be sure to break in any new boots before the hunt.

If you shoot a big game animal, approach it cautiously from behind. Tap the carcass with your foot and be ready to shoot if the animal reacts. Stay away from the rear hooves. Even if the animal appears dead it may kick out of reflex.

Field dress the animal immediately by removing the entrails and windpipe. Begin cooling the carcass as soon as possible. Skinning and hanging the animal will speed the cooling process. You may have to cut up large animals, like moose or elk. Because of its bulk, the whole carcass may retain body heat too long, spoiling the meat. If you must use a bone saw, be extremely careful to keep bits of fat and bone marrow off the meat. They can affect its taste.

Place a rope around the dead animal's neck to drag it out. If the animal is too large to drag, cut it into pieces and carry them out on a packframe. You can also debone the meat to reduce weight.

If the animal has exceptionally large antlers or horns, you may want to have them measured for possible record status. Take precautions so you do not damage the tines or split the skull plate when removing the rack, or when dragging or transporting the carcass. Check with your state wildlife agency for instructions on obtaining an official score. The Boone and Crockett Club keeps records for trophy animals killed with firearms; the Pope and Young Club for big game killed with bow and arrow.

EQUIPMENT for big game hunting includes: (1) wrist compass, (2) all-purpose folding knife and (3) small binoculars, items that fit inside a shirt or pants pocket. Inside a rucksack, carry a (4) regular-sized binoculars, (5) extra compass, (6) skinning knife with rounded blade, (7) canteen, (8) flashlight, (9) space blanket, (10) small mirror for emergency signalling, (11) waterproof matches, (12) tow rope, (13) candy bars, (14) freeze-dried food. Use the (15) stout cord for tying up a (16) space blanket tarp for temporary shelter.

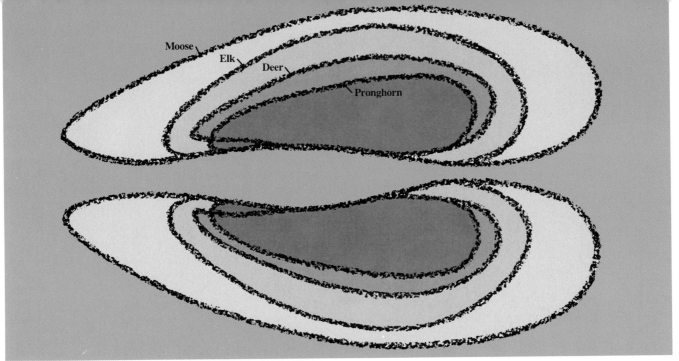

TRACKS of adult big game animals vary in size and shape. Moose tracks measure about 5 to 7 inches long; elk tracks 3½ to 5 inches. A moose track is more pointed than that of an elk. Deer tracks range from 2½ to 3½ inches long. Pronghorn tracks approach the size of deer tracks, but have straighter outside edges.

SHOOT for the heart-lung area (shaded) of a big game animal. The best shot is directly from the side, where the most vital area is exposed. When an animal is quartering toward the hunter, slightly more than half as much vital area is vulnerable; slightly less than half when quartering away. An animal facing the hunter has only a small part of the vital area exposed. Facing away, none of the vital area is vulnerable and the shot would damage too much meat.

TYPICAL ANTLERS are fairly symmetrical, although they sometimes have a different number of tines on each side. But abnormal tines and differences between the two antlers in tine count or size of the main beam will lower the official score of the rack.

NON-TYPICAL ANTLERS can be almost symmetrical or extremely asymmetrical. Many have a large number of oddly-shaped tines in unusual locations. Some have tines that point downward. Abnormal points add to the score of non-typical racks.

White-tailed Deer

The whitetail rates as the number one big game animal in North America. Hunters who pursue all types of big game consider a whitetail buck to be the supreme challenge.

Whitetails test a hunter's skill because of their elusive nature. In a Michigan experiment, 39 deer including 7 bucks, 14 does and 18 fawns were fenced inside a 1-square-mile area. Six experienced hunters attempted to find the deer. On the fourth day, one hunter finally spotted a buck. After one month, the average amount of time needed for a hunter to spot a buck was 51 hours. It took an average of 14 hours to spot any deer.

This amazing ability to elude hunters results from the whitetail's keen senses, its ability to hide, and its intimate knowledge of its home range.

Whitetails rely mainly on their sense of smell to detect danger. They can catch a whiff of human scent from blocks away. Deer also hear extremely well. They do not have particularly sharp eyesight, but are quick to detect lateral movement. Deer were once thought to be color blind, but researchers have discovered that deer can perceive some color.

Most hunters find it hard to believe they could walk by a deer only a few feet away. But whitetails regularly elude hunters by sitting tight in grassy or brushy cover. Their coats blend in perfectly.

Deer are so familiar with their surroundings that they can quickly find an escape route or patch of cover. And they are sure to notice any change in their surroundings, like a new deer stand. They will avoid the area for several days until they get used to the new feature.

Whitetails usually attempt to escape danger by sneaking away unnoticed. When alarmed, bucks and does may snort loudly and stamp their feet. This serves as a warning to other deer. If threatened, a deer will bound away with its snowy white tail, or *flag*, erect. But they normally run only a short distance, then look back to see if they are being pursued. If not, they resume their normal activity.

Deer can attain speeds of 35 to 40 miles-per-hour and easily jump an 8-foot barrier. If they cannot escape by land, they will take to water. Whitetails are strong swimmers, and have been observed crossing lakes several miles wide.

A whitetail's coat is reddish-brown in spring and summer, and brown or gray from fall through winter. Although the underside of the tail is white, the outside is the same color as the rest of the coat and covers up the white rump.

More than two dozen varieties of whitetails inhabit North America. The smallest variety is the Key deer, which generally weighs from 45 to 65 pounds. It lives only in the Florida Keys. The largest variety, the northern white-tailed deer, usually weighs from 130 to 190 pounds. It is found in the northeastern states and into southern Canada. The heaviest whitetail on record, 511 pounds, was shot in Minnesota in 1926.

The life-span of a whitetail seldom exceeds 8 years. Most deer taken by hunters are 1½ or 2½ years old. You cannot tell a whitetail's age by its antlers. A 1½-year-old buck may have only spikes, or it may have three or four points per side. Older bucks usually have four points on a side, but sometimes as many as seven.

The record whitetail rack came from a Wisconsin deer shot in 1914. Each antler has five points and measures 30 inches long. The spread between the antlers is 20⅛ inches.

Whitetails feed primarily on buds and twigs from shrubs and small trees. They also graze on grasses, clover, and other green plants. In agricultural areas, they commonly feed on alfalfa, oats, wheat and corn, but will eat almost any crop available.

Does spend the summer and fall with one or two fawns. Mature bucks live alone, except during the breeding season. Whitetails mate between October and January. The rutting period lasts longer in the South than it does in the North. During the early stages of the rut, both bucks and does become less cautious. Bucks are busy making scrapes to advertise their presence to does. The does move from one scrape to another looking for a suitable mate.

White-tailed Deer
Range

Where to Find Whitetails

Whitetails can be found from the conifer forests of Canada to the chaparral plains of Mexico. No other big game animal can adapt to such a diversity of habitat. The whitetail thrives in farmlands, in city suburbs, and other areas where human development has severely reduced or eliminated populations of other big game.

Young hardwood forests make prime habitat. Whitetails prefer large woodlands, but can survive in smaller areas like woodlots and tree-lined stream corridors. Deer also live in grasslands, brushlands and swamps.

If you locate a good whitetail area when scouting before the season, chances are the deer will be there when the season begins. Whitetails have a surprisingly small home range. In a Texas study, marked deer were observed over a 5-year period. On the average, does remained within a ⅙-square-mile area. Bucks ranged much more, but stayed within an area averaging 1⅔ square miles

Your best chance of seeing whitetails is during feeding periods or when they move between resting and feeding areas. Deer feed most heavily before sunrise and after sunset. They bed down in midday. But season, weather, moon phase, and hunting pressure can alter daily movements.

The changing seasons can affect whitetail movements in several ways. As the weather begins to cool in fall, deer feed for longer periods to build up their fat reserves for winter. When the acorns start to fall, deer often feed in the woods rather than moving to their usual feeding areas. Movement increases during the rutting period, as deer wander about in search of a mate.

Changing weather usually increases deer movement. The animals sense impending weather changes, so they feed heavily while they can. On hot, sunny days, deer spend more time bedded down. They do not necessarily seek cover during a light drizzle. In fact, they often stand out in the open rather than lie in wet grass. But a heavy rain will force them into dense cover, like conifer stands.

During a full moon, whitetails may not come out to feed until after dark. In the dark phase, deer begin feeding earlier. They do not feed as heavily at night, because the lack of light curtails their activity.

Hunting pressure can have a dramatic effect on deer movements. In heavily-hunted areas, whitetails change their feeding schedule once the season begins. They feed earlier and later in the day, or even at night, to avoid exposing themselves to hunters during shooting hours.

Typical Whitetail Habitat

HARDWOOD FORESTS provide food and cover. A young forest is best, because sunlight can reach the forest floor to grow shrubs and grasses.

FARMLANDS offer ample food supplies. They can support large numbers of deer if they have cover like brushy draws or stream corridors.

LOWLANDS like swamps, bogs and river bottoms provide dense cover. Whitetails usually feed in surrounding fields or woodlands.

DAILY MOVEMENTS during fall normally begin when deer move into feeding areas like (1) brushy edges, (2) harvested rowcrops, (3) hayfields and (4) fields of green vegetation. They feed until about sunrise, then move to loafing cover like (5) clumps of trees and brush. Or they may retreat to heavier cover like (6) woodlots and (7) wooded creek bottoms. In late afternoon, they return to feeding areas where they stay until after sunset. When heavily hunted, deer sometimes lie in the middle of (8) large, plowed fields where they can see hunters easily.

Signs of Whitetail Activity

RUBS on small saplings result from bucks marking their territories by rubbing scent from glands on top of their heads. Bucks rub dozens of trees during the rut, seldom returning to the same ones. They also rub before the rut to remove velvet from their antlers.

SCRAPES on the ground mean that a buck is attempting to attract does. As they paw the ground, whitetail bucks often thrash nearby saplings or overhanging branches with their antlers. They check their scrapes regularly, especially those visited by does.

Tips for Finding Whitetails

TRACKS AND DROPPINGS reveal how many deer are using an area. Whitetail pellets are more elongated than those of rabbits and hares.

DAY TRAILS wind through thick brush and trees, but seldom cross clearings. Hunters wait along these trails when deer are most active.

NIGHT TRAILS lead through meadows or open croplands. Do not choose a stand along this type of trail, because deer seldom use them in daylight.

RATTLING draws bucks during the rut. Take a stand near a dense thicket where you spotted deer the previous day. Or rattle near a fresh scrape, if the spot offers a clear shot. Rub, knock and rattle two antlers together to imitate the sound of fighting bucks. If nothing appears within 15 to 30 minutes, move quietly to another spot.

Hunting for Whitetails

Hunters use dozens of techniques to outwit whitetails. Stand-hunting, still-hunting and driving account for the vast majority of deer. But stalking, float-hunting and even unusual methods like antler rattling can be effective.

You can greatly improve your chances by planning your hunt weeks before the season opens. It is possible for an opening-day hunter to leisurely walk into the forest, find a likely-looking spot, and bag a trophy buck within minutes. But the odds against such a chance encounter are staggering.

Hunters who enjoy consistent success invest a great deal of time in pre-season scouting. Regardless of how good a spot was in previous years, make sure it still holds good numbers of deer. If you find little sign, look somewhere else. Once you locate a likely area, examine it closely to determine movement paths and escape routes.

Expert deer hunters know not only where, but when to hunt. Wind is an important consideration. You can approach deer more easily if a light breeze rustles the leaves. This background noise makes the sound of your footsteps less noticeable. In a strong wind, deer bed down in cover and stay extra-alert.

Some hunters prefer a light rain because it softens the leaves and twigs so they do not crackle underfoot. A light rain provides a low level of background noise, but does not reduce deer activity. In a heavy rain, the animals bed down under dense, overhead cover. Powdery snow makes for quiet walking and good tracking. But when a hard crust develops, deer can hear you coming. Snow-covered tree boughs muffle your sound and may block a deer's vision.

Temperature and cloud cover also affect hunting success, but not the way many hunters think. The common belief is that hunting is best on cool or cloudy days. But after thousands of hours of observation, members of a nationwide hunting club found that deer move about more when the weather is warm rather than cold; clear rather than cloudy.

Some hunters use bottled scents, either to mask their own odor or to attract deer. Masking scents are made with skunk or fox urine and sprinkled around the stand. Attractants, made from the urine of a doe in heat or various fruits, are spread in the area where you want to shoot your deer.

You do not need high-velocity cartridges for whitetails, because most shots are at close range. Cartridges should be a minimum of .240 caliber with bullets at least 100 grains.

Stand-hunting for Whitetails

Whitetails are creatures of habit. If you have scouted an area thoroughly and selected a stand near signs of recent deer activity, you can be sure that whitetails will eventually pass your way. If you lose confidence, become impatient and decide to go after the deer, you significantly reduce your odds.

Choose a stand that offers good visibility. It should be located where the wind will not blow your scent toward a trail or other spot where you expect to see deer. You should also select a spot where the sun will not shine in your eyes. Be sure you are concealed on the sides from which deer will most likely approach.

But deer may not come from the direction you expect, so you must slowly scan in a complete circle around your stand. When you spot a deer at a distance, stay motionless and be patient. If you see a doe, watch closely because there may be a buck trailing behind.

If you hunt in the morning, walk to your stand very quietly. Be sure to get there while it is still dark. Most hunters stay at their stand until about two hours after sunrise. But it often pays to wait a little longer. The commotion caused by other hunters leaving their stands may spook deer to you. If you hunt in the afternoon, stay until the close of shooting hours. Hunters often see more deer in the final minutes than during the rest of the day.

ELEVATED STANDS place you above a deer's usual vision level. They also expand your field of view and keep your scent above the ground. But many hunters simply hide behind a tree, or a pile of logs or brush.

Tips for Stand-hunting

INTERSECTIONS of two or more heavily-used trails make prime stand-hunting locations. Another good spot is an area with many fresh scrapes.

OUTSIDE BENDS along trails are also good stand sites. They enable you to see deer coming from a long distance in either direction.

TOWER BLINDS make it possible to hunt from a high elevation where there are no tall trees. Most tower blinds are permanent.

Still-hunting for Whitetails

Of all the whitetail hunting techniques, still-hunting is the most difficult to master. But the challenge of trying to find a weak spot in the deer's ironclad defense system appeals to many hunters.

Still-hunting works best during midday, when whitetails are loafing or bedded down. Most hunters prefer damp weather and a light wind to obscure the sound of their footsteps.

The slower you move, the more deer you will see. Place each step carefully; plant your toe first, then gradually lower your heel. Try to avoid twigs and leaves. Stop after a few steps, then slowly move your head to examine the terrain. Bend down from time to time to scan the ground below the leaf line.

If you accidentally make a noise, stop moving immediately. If they do not detect motion, whitetails will usually forget the disturbance within a few minutes. Many hunters prefer to still-hunt on trails because they can move more quietly. Most trails are packed down, so you do not crunch leaves. They also have less brush to scrape against your clothes.

Always walk against the wind so your scent does not precede you through the woods. This method will also help you sneak up on feeding deer. They usually face into the wind and will not see you coming.

LOOK for signs like the flick of an ear, the glint off an antler, or the white throat patch of a deer. A bedded whitetail will often sit tight while a hunter passes within a few yards.

WALK across rows of standing corn, peeking both ways down each row. Whitetails often feed and bed in standing rowcrops. The technique works best on breezy days; the rustling stalks prevent deer from hearing you.

Driving for Whitetails

The success of a deer drive depends on good organization. A group of hunters wandering haphazardly through the woods has little hope of shooting deer.

Every drive should have a leader who is familiar with the terrain. Before the drive, the leader gives clear instructions to each hunter. Posters take their stands first; each should wait in a spot with a good view, preferably from an elevated stand. Drivers synchronize their watches, then spread out across the upwind side of cover. Distance between the drivers may be only 15 yards in dense cover or more than 50 yards if the cover is sparse.

At the appointed time, drivers begin walking downwind. Deer soon detect the hunter's scent. They will flush closer if drivers move quietly. Some deer move ahead, some double back, and others remain bedded down.

Driving will work anytime deer are in cover. But if you drive a block of cover too large, deer will slip to the side and let the drivers pass.

Deer drives can be dangerous. Limit the number of hunters so you can keep track of everyone's location. Posters in elevated stands also make a drive safer. Their shots angle toward the ground, and they are above the normal shooting plane of the drivers.

WATCH closely for whitetails doubling back through the driving line. Deer may sneak back even though drivers are visible on both sides. As drivers approach posters, deer must double back or break into the open.

KEEP adjacent drivers in sight at all times. This prevents a hunter from moving too far ahead of the others and into the firing zone.

POST near a known escape route. Deer often move from one block of woods to another by sneaking through a connecting patch of lighter cover.

FLUSH deer from dense cover with a confusion drive. Drivers blow whistles or yell to roust bedded deer and to keep them from doubling back.

Mule Deer

The mule deer's popularity is unrivaled among western big game. The animal is named for its mule-like ears, which may measure a foot long. Muleys look much like whitetails, but differ greatly in behavior and personality.

You can tell a mule deer from a whitetail by the black tip on its tail. Most of the muley's tail is white, making the rump patch more evident than it is on whitetails. Their antlers also differ. The main beam of a mule deer antler is forked; whitetails have a continuous main beam.

The record mule deer rack has a spread of 30⅞ inches. Its right antler has six points and a main beam that measures 30⅛ inches long; its left has five points and totals 28¾ inches. The animal was shot in Colorado in 1972.

Like whitetails, mule deer have excellent senses of smell and hearing. But muleys have better long-distance vision. They usually bed down where they have a good view of the surrounding terrain. Unlike whitetails, they rarely sit tight and let hunters pass only yards away.

When they detect something unusual, mule deer cock their large ears to pinpoint the direction of the disturbance. Then they bound off in pogo-stick fashion, with all four feet touching the ground simultaneously. This distinctive gait, called *stotting*, enables them to survey the terrain better and to change direction instantly.

A startled mule deer will run much farther than a whitetail, sometimes up to four miles. They usually bound uphill, often pausing for a last look before slipping over a ridge. Muleys normally run with their tails down.

Compared to whitetails, mule deer have a calm disposition. They show little fear of man as long as enough distance separates them. But they become nervous and often slip away when a hunter disappears from sight.

Mule deer prefer terrain more open than that used by whitetails. Mountains and foothills with sparse stands of timber, rolling prairies broken by canyons and coulees, and low brushlands make ideal habitat.

Where mule deer and whitetails co-exist, they eat many of the same foods. But the mule deer's diet usually differs because of the rougher terrain. Common foods include bitterbrush, mountain mahogany, serviceberry, chokecherry and sagebrush.

Early morning and late afternoon are the prime feeding periods of mule deer. Favorite areas are brushy hillsides, meadows, croplands and pastures, generally at lower elevations than bedding areas.

Mule deer move as much as 2 miles from feeding to bedding areas. In midday, they often bed down on the lee side of a break. They may rest just below the crest of a hill or the lip of a ravine. They watch only the downhill side, relying on the wind to bring them the scent of anything approaching from behind. Mule deer will also bed on a grassy mountain terrace, in the bottom of a dry wash, or near a tree on a hillside. In remote areas, they may feed in the open rather than bed down during the day.

After a rainy period, look for mule deer on sunny hillsides. Heavy snow drives them from the mountains to lower ground. Herds migrate as far as 50 miles, often wintering in brushy draws and canyons, blown free of snow.

Mule deer often form large herds. Small and medium-sized bucks mix with does and fawns, but the largest bucks are usually loners.

Most mule deer breed in November and December, but the breeding period may be as early as October or as late as March. During the rut, the bucks thrash or *horn* bushes, poles, branches and tree trunks in a display of dominance. They do not make scrapes.

Seven varieties of mule deer inhabit the western third of North America. The desert mule deer ranges as far south as central Mexico. The most numerous variety, the Rocky Mountain mule deer, is found as far north as the Northwest Territories.

Rocky Mountain mule deer reach the largest size, generally weighing from 140 to 200 pounds. The largest on record, 453 pounds, was taken in Montana. The southern mule deer is the smallest variety; it weighs from 85 to 110 pounds.

Black-tailed deer, although closely related to mule deer, are darker, generally smaller, and have ears only 6 to 7 inches long. They live in steep, heavily-forested terrain along the Pacific Coast. They behave more like whitetails.

Mule Deer Range

MULE DEER antlers are generally taller and have a greater spread than those of white-tailed deer. On a good-sized mule deer, each fork will branch again for a minimum of four points per side.

TAIL COLOR distinguishes the black-tailed deer from mule deer. On a blacktail (left), the entire outside of the tail is black. On mule deer, only the tip is black.

DAILY MOVEMENTS usually begin with mule deer moving to feeding areas like (1) a grassy stream margin in a ravine. They feed until 1 to 2 hours after sunrise, then bed in areas like (2) a ledge near the top of the ravine. Large bucks may bed on (3) rocky terraces at higher elevation. Deer return to feeding areas about an hour before sunset.

GLASS potential feeding and bedding areas with binoculars. A spotting scope works better for long distances. Look for a reflection off shiny antlers; buff-white patches of throat or rump hair; or the symmetrical shape of a mule deer's face and ears, which resembles a three-bladed propeller (inset).

Hunting for Mule Deer

Most hunters find it easier to outsmart a mule deer than a whitetail. The muley's less secretive nature and penchant for open terrain often tip the scales in favor of the hunter. But a big buck mule deer can be just as elusive as a trophy whitetail.

When hunting in hilly or mountainous terrain, get to the highest part of your hunting area early in the morning, preferably before shooting hours. Your chances of spotting muleys in the open are best in the morning, and the high elevation gives you a good view.

Glass every detail of the landscape. Mule deer blend in well with their surroundings and are masters at concealing themselves in a small amount of cover. If you spot one animal, look closely for others because mule deer often feed and bed in groups.

If the animal is too far away for a shot, plan a stalk. Use natural features of the landscape, like ravines, for concealment. Try to approach from above, because muleys expect danger from below.

Should glassing prove futile, begin still-hunting your way downhill. Some hunters take stands along trails where muleys are likely to pass. When hunting with companions, driving can be effective.

A running mule deer makes a difficult target because of its bounding gait and unpredictable turns. But it may stop and look back if you shout or whistle. Be ready for a standing shot as it nears the top of a ridge or a stand of timber. A muley will often stop just before it disappears.

Mule deer hunters take shots up to 300 yards, so sight in your rifle for long-range shooting. Use a high-velocity cartridge of at least .240 caliber with a minimum bullet weight of 80 grains.

STILL-HUNT a series of ravines by starting at the head of one ravine, then walking the edge (dotted line). Look over the crest periodically to spot bedded deer. Cross the ravine at the lower end and walk the other side to check for deer you may have missed. Then, cross to the head of the next ravine and repeat the procedure.

STAND-HUNT along corridors between feeding and bedding areas. Conceal yourself behind a natural feature like a rock outcrop or large tree, or use a tree stand. Mule deer trails are usually less distinct than those of whitetails. But the animals often follow natural passes like a saddle between two ridges.

How to Drive for Mule Deer

DRIVE for mule deer in ravines. One hunter walks up the bottom and another halfway up the side. A third hunter posts at the head of the ravine. Driving also works well along wooded or brushy stream corridors.

WATCH for mule deer heading uphill as the drive progresses. Drivers should shoot before deer reach the top of the ridge. The poster may get a shot at deer trying to escape out the head of the ravine.

Elk

Prized for its magnificent antlers and delectable meat, a bull elk is the big game hunter's greatest trophy. A large animal may have antlers five feet long.

Antlers of the largest bulls, called *monarchs*, have eight points on a side. *Imperial* elk have seven points per side, and *royal* elk six. The record elk rack has eight points on one side and seven on the other. The main beam of one antler measures 59⅝ inches; the other 55⅝ inches. The rack, which has a 45½-inch spread, came from an elk taken in Colorado in 1899.

Two varieties of elk provide the vast majority of hunting. Most numerous is the Rocky Mountain elk. The slightly larger Roosevelt elk lives in the coastal mountains of the Pacific Northwest. Elk are brownish-gray with long, chestnut-brown hair on the neck. The tail and rump patch are buff-white. Bulls average about 750 pounds and stand 5 feet high at the shoulder. Cows weigh about one-fourth less.

Elk prefer heavily-timbered country broken by clearcuts, burns, and meadows, called *parks*. The best habitat is in remote, mountainous terrain laced with streams and small glacial lakes. Elk have large territories and will not tolerate human disturbance.

Cow elk live in large herds which also include calves and an occasional spike bull. An old cow leads the herd, alerting the others to danger with a sharp bark. Older bulls live alone or in small groups of up to six. Bulls wander more than cows, shunning cow herds until the mating season.

The rut usually begins in early September. A dominant bull, called a *herd bull*, assembles a harem of up to 30 cows. He protects them from the advances of younger males, or of other herd bulls.

To detect danger, elk rely mainly on a keen sense of smell. They also have excellent hearing. On windy days, when swishing tree limbs would obscure the sound of a hunter's approach, they become nervous and retreat to heavy cover. Elk quickly notice movement, but usually ignore stationary objects.

An elk can run 35 miles-per-hour in a short burst and can maintain a 15 to 20 miles-per-hour trot over a long distance. A running bull carries his nose high, so his antlers lay back along his body and do not tangle in branches. Elk are strong swimmers and can jump obstructions up to 10 feet high.

Elk feed mainly on grasses. As winter nears, they consume more twigs and leaves from shrubs and trees. The morning feeding period begins about one hour before sunrise and lasts until one hour after. In late afternoon, they begin feeding about two hours before sunset and continue until dark. Elk usually have four or five shorter feeding periods during the day, each lasting from 15 minutes to one hour. Because they eat so often, elk usually bed within a mile of where they feed. They prefer bedding areas with a good view, like a grassy terrace on a hillside.

In summer and early fall, elk scatter over a large area at high elevation. The rugged terrain prevents intrusion by humans. In late fall, heavy snow and extreme cold push elk to lower elevations. But with a break in the weather, they may return to high altitudes. Some herds move 100 miles to find the right conditions.

Elk Range

Signs of Elk Activity

DROPPINGS that are elongated and ¾ to 1½ inches in length mean that elk have been browsing on twigs and leaves. Droppings in a large mass are from elk that have eaten green grass.

WALLOWS are made by big bulls to announce their presence to cows. A bull scrapes out a depression at a spring seep. He urinates in the mud, then rolls in it, plastering his body.

FRESH RUBS during the rut also advertise a large bull's presence. Elk rubs are higher than those made by deer, and the bark of the sapling is stripped over a greater length.

84

BUGLING takes place during the rut. It consists of a series of melodious whistles, progressing from a low to high pitch. Herd bulls bugle to intimidate competing males. Challengers bugle to lure the herd bull away from his harem. In addition to bugling, herd bulls bellow, rake trees with their antlers, and spar with other bulls to drive them off. Occasionally, two bulls ram each other and lock antlers in a test of strength.

DAILY MOVEMENT patterns depend on hunting pressure. When not disturbed, elk feed in (1) open meadows or (2) areas with young trees and shrubs. They bed down at (3) the edge of timber nearby. If threatened, they move up to 5 miles into the timber after feeding. Or they may retreat to (4) a steep, conifer-studded slope where they sniff rising air currents to detect danger from below.

MIGRATIONS in late fall begin when snow depth reaches 18 inches or more, and temperatures plunge below zero. Elk move to snow-free, south-facing slopes at lower elevations.

85

Hunting for Elk

PACK TRAINS enable hunters to reach the remote, mountainous areas which offer the best elk hunting. Horses or mules also simplify the task of carrying out the antlers and cut-up carcasses.

A successful elk hunter must earn his trophy. Unlike most other big game animals, elk will retreat deep into the forest or climb to extreme elevations to escape hunting pressure. Seldom can you drive to your hunting area and hope to bag an elk.

Elk hunters often spend several days in the mountains. They scout a prospective area to find fresh elk sign, then set up camp at least one-half mile away.

Scent helps hunters locate areas used by elk. The animals emit a strong, musky odor, similar to the smell of sheep. The scent lingers in bedding or wallowing areas long after the elk leave.

One of the most productive techniques is stand-hunting in early morning and late afternoon. For a

How to Call In a Bull Elk

CALLS include: (1) flute, (2) pigtail and (3) tube types. Diaphragm calls (4) mimic small, medium and old bulls. Tapes (5) help you learn the best calls.

BUGLE for elk starting at dawn. When a bull answers, move toward him, staying downwind and calling about every five minutes as long as he continues to respond. Keep approaching until you get within about 400 yards. Then, select a blind and continue calling to lure him within shooting range.

86

morning hunt, walk to your stand in the dark, moving quietly to avoid spooking any elk in the vicinity. Remain on your stand until about two hours after sunrise, glassing to find elk that you could stalk. In the afternoon, be on your stand at least two hours before sunset.

In midday, when elk are bedded down, you are more likely to see them by still-hunting. The technique works best when the ground is damp or covered with soft snow. In a dry woods, it is nearly impossible to walk quietly enough to approach within gun range.

Driving can also be effective, but only if your hunting party is familiar with the terrain. Drivers approach from below a known bedding area and push the elk uphill to posters. The posters station themselves along game trails in thick timber or near clearings where elk are likely to break into the open. A startled elk will make plenty of noise. But more often, they slip away silently, so posters must watch closely.

During the rut, hunters can bugle in bull elk. Many elk calls mimic the high-pitched, squeaky whistle of a spike bull. This call infuriates the herd bull. He thinks an unworthy youngster is making a play for his harem, so he moves toward the caller, ready to do battle. If a bull answers but does not move, he is probably guarding his harem and reluctant to leave. In this case, try stalking close enough for a shot.

Because elk are so large and shooting distances so long, most hunters prefer high-velocity cartridges of .270 caliber or larger. Use a bullet weighing at least 150 grains.

Other Elk Hunting Techniques

STAND-HUNT above trails or wallows, or at the edge of a meadow where elk feed. Trails and feeding areas are most productive in early morning and late afternoon. Bulls usually visit wallows late in the day.

STILL-HUNT to within shooting range. Bowhunters often get as close as 20 yards. Start by walking a ridge, looking for elk on terraces or hillsides. Approach elk from above because they usually watch the downhill side.

FOLLOW fresh elk tracks in the snow. Stay on the trail as long as it goes downhill; stay above the trail if it moves across the slope. Constantly look ahead so you see the animal before it sees you.

Moose

With antlers towering 10 feet above the ground, a bull moose is truly an awesome sight. A large bull weighs 1200 pounds and moose up to 1800 pounds have been recorded. The world-record rack has a 77-inch spread. The right *palm* measures 49⅝ inches and has 18 points; the left 49¾ inches with 16 points.

Like other members of the deer family, moose have an excellent sense of smell and good hearing. But their eyesight is poorer than that of deer. Moose seldom notice a nearby hunter if he does not move.

Despite their size, moose can run up to 30 miles-per-hour. When spooked, they will crash through brush and small trees, ignoring trails. But moose can also slip quietly through cover to elude a hunter.

Young hardwood forests with scattered conifers, and brushy lowlands make ideal moose habitat. The dense undergrowth provides ample food and bedding cover. But they can also live in older forests with little underbrush.

A big bull can browse on vegetation up to 11 feet off the ground. If it cannot reach the upper portion of a small tree, a moose will straddle the trunk, then start walking. The animal bends down the tree, feeding on leaves and twigs as it walks.

Moose feed most heavily from just before sunrise to about two hours after, and again in late afternoon. But they may feed anytime during the day or night. When not feeding, moose bed down in thickets.

Most of the year, moose live by themselves. They lead docile lives, seldom moving more than one-half mile in a day. But during the rut, which begins in September, bulls become ill-tempered. They have

MOOSE have a dark brown, almost black, coat. A large bull stands 7 feet tall at the shoulder and measures 10 feet in length. Each antler has a large palm with numerous points along the outer edge. Moose usually stay near water. Bogs and lakes provide a source of food, a place to cool off and a refuge from swarms of insects. Excellent swimmers, moose will not hesitate to cross a fast river or even a large lake.

been known to attack cars and even trains. Rutting bulls regularly visit wallows. Both sexes roam widely during the rut, sometimes wandering over 10 miles from their usual home range.

Hunters see the most moose on clear, calm days. Heavy overcast, rain, snow or high winds keep the animals bedded down.

Before you hunt, scout the area for sign. With animals of this size, the evidence will be obvious. Select a stand near a wallow, a well-used stream crossing, or any spot where the topography funnels moose through a small area. Get to your stand before daylight, remain until mid-morning, then return in late afternoon.

Still-hunting can be effective in midday, especially if there is snow to quiet your footsteps. If you attempt to sneak through heavy timber and brush, you will make too much noise. During the rut, antler rattling

or calling may lure bulls from dense cover. Using cupped hands or a birchbark megaphone, make a series of short grunts to imitate a cow in heat. If you hear a response, pour water in a puddle to imitate a cow urinating.

In hilly or mountainous country, hunters stalk moose after spotting them with binoculars. Float-hunting works well along streams and lakeshores.

Moose Range

Most moose hunters use large-caliber rifles and high-velocity ammunition, similar to those used for elk. A moose may not drop immediately after the shot. To prevent losing a wounded animal, wait 10 to 15 minutes for it to lie down, then begin pursuing it.

Tips for Finding Moose

BROKEN SAPLINGS indicate a bull moose in rut. A bull twists off saplings with his antlers to advertise his presence to cows.

DROPPINGS measure 1 to 1½ inches long. When moose are eating browse, droppings have a consistency similar to compressed sawdust.

BRUSHY LOWLANDS are favorite feeding areas. Moose prefer red-osier dogwood, willow, aspen, birch, mountain ash and aquatic plants.

Moose Hunting Techniques

GLASS for moose along forest edges, in willow swamps or near other feeding areas. Get to your vantage point early, so you can complete your stalk before the animals retreat to bedding areas.

FLOAT-HUNT for moose if preliminary scouting shows abundant sign along the streambank. The technique works best in early morning and late afternoon, when moose come to drink and to feed on shoreline willows.

Pronghorns

The pronghorn's astonishing speed and superb eyesight are unmatched among North American big game. Hunters refer to pronghorns as antelope, but they are not related to the antelope of Africa.

Pronghorns get their name from the sharp prongs that project forward on the horns of bucks. Their upper body is tan; the underside and rump white. Most antelope weigh 80 to 130 pounds, with the largest bucks weighing up to 140. The record pronghorn rack has a right horn measuring 18⅛ inches in length and a prong of 7¾ inches. Its left horn totals 18¼ inches with a 7¼-inch prong. The animal was shot in Arizona in 1975.

The fleet-footed pronghorn can reach a speed of 60 miles-per-hour. Its vision compares to that of a hu-man using 8x binoculars. The pronghorn's large, protruding eyes give it an exceptionally wide field of view.

Pronghorns prefer open plains, prairies, and tree-less foothills. The best country has rolling hills sprin-kled with water holes and ample sagebrush for food. Pronghorns also eat forbs, brush and occasionally grasses. They feed most heavily in early morning and late afternoon, but may graze anytime day or night. They usually head to water in mid-morning.

During the hunting season, pronghorns live in herds numbering from a few to several dozen animals. A typical herd consists mainly of does and fawns with one dominant buck and a few smaller bucks. Some-times several bucks band together. The largest bucks live alone, often in rugged terrain.

Pronghorns maintain a constant vigil to spot danger. A herd often has a sentry doe that keeps watch from a knoll. When alarmed, an antelope flares its white rump hairs, alerting others in the herd. Despite their

LOCATE pronghorns by glassing from a ridge. Sneak quietly to the edge, because there may be antelope on the other side. Use a spotting scope to check horn length.

IDENTIFY bucks by their black cheek patch. Mature bucks have horns that extend above the ears. Some does have buttons or spikes, but they are shorter than the ears.

nervous nature, they are curious and often investigate unusual sights and sounds.

Rutting begins in late August or early September. Bucks gather a harem and vigorously defend it against intruding bucks. They butt heads and slash with their horns to settle differences. Sometimes the herd buck shows off by making sideways leaps and running in circles. These antics may distract does, improving your chances of stalking close enough for a shot.

When not disturbed, pronghorns usually stay within a one-square-mile area. But during the hunting season, they often run five miles or more to escape danger. Antelope could easily jump a fence, but seldom do. They crawl under or hop through barbed wire fences, but woven wire usually blocks their movement.

Searching for sign is a waste of time. You can see the animals simply by looking for spots of white. Many hunters locate herds by driving ranch roads. If you spot a herd from a moving vehicle, do not change speed. Instead, drive until out of sight of the animals, then stop to plan your strategy. If it is too late in the day to start a stalk, wait until the next morning and begin glassing at sun-up. Study the terrain to determine the best stalking route.

Stalking pronghorns on flat terrain is difficult. Instead, take a stand where the animals may come close enough for a shot. Other hunters sometimes move to the opposite side of the herd to drive the animals toward the stander.

Pronghorn Range

Antelope hunters use rifles and ammunition like those used for mule deer. Variable scopes are ideal. You can increase the power for long shots, which may exceed 300 yards, or decrease it for close or moving targets.

STALK to within shooting range by creeping just below a rise. Grass or brush will break up your outline.

STAND-HUNT from a hay-bale blind near a water hole or fence crossing. Or simply hide in a depression.

LURE antelope closer by waving a cloth or hat. Or blow a predator call. These tactics appeal to their curiosity.

Black Bear

Of all big game animals, bear are the most misunderstood. Some people regard them as fun-loving clowns. Others envision them as bloodthirsty killers. Records exist of black bear attacking humans, but they usually make every effort to avoid man.

Black bear favor mixed conifer and hardwood forests, with clearings that produce food. A bear's diet consists mainly of berries, fruits, nuts, grasses, corn and other crops. But they also eat insects, small mammals and fish. In spring, they may feed on carcasses of animals killed by severe winter weather. They frequently gorge themselves at garbage dumps. Bear have an enormous appetite in late summer and fall. They often gain over 100 pounds in preparation for hibernation.

Bear feed most heavily during cool morning and evening hours. They remain in shady areas on hot days because their dark fur absorbs too much heat from the sun. Windy or rainy weather also reduces their activity.

With the exception of the June breeding season, males, or *boars,* lead solitary lives. *Sows* stay with cubs for about 1½ years. Boars have a much larger territory than sows, often over 100 square miles.

In the North, bear begin hibernating as early as mid-September. They remain in their dens until April, although they occasionally wander about during a warm spell. In warmer climates, bear may not hibernate. If they do, hibernation begins later and does not last as long.

Black bear have many color phases. Most are glossy black, brown, or cinnamon, but they may be white or even bluish. A large boar weighs 300 to 400 pounds; some exceed 600. Sows weigh about one-third less. The largest black bear on record weighed 802 pounds. It was taken in Wisconsin in 1885.

Biologists rate the bear among the most intelligent game animals. A bear can run 25 miles-per-hour and climb a tree in seconds. They rely mainly on a keen sense of smell to find food and detect danger. They have excellent hearing, but poor eyesight.

Even in good bear country, the animals are not abundant, averaging only one bear for every two square miles. Because bear are so scattered, hunters employ techniques seldom used for other big game.

Baiting takes advantage of the bear's highly-developed sense of smell. A bear can detect the scent of bait from over one-half mile away and will come to the hunter's stand. This method works in spring when hungry bear emerge from dens, and in fall when they feed heavily to build up fat reserves.

Some bear hunters use hounds, such as Walkers, black-and-tans, or Plotts. But many people consider the use of dogs unsporting, and in some states it is illegal. Those who object maintain that the bear has no chance. In reality, however, it often wins. A bear can run for miles and often loses the dogs. When cornered, it can quickly dispatch a hound. Some hunters pursue bear solely for the sport of the chase. Once an animal is treed or brought to bay, they call off the dogs and let it go.

Still-hunting in feeding areas accounts for some bear, but the odds of randomly walking up on an animal are slim. They are too wary and their populations too sparse.

Bear hunters use rifles of at least .30 caliber. You can kill a bear with a smaller caliber, but a larger caliber reduces the chances of a bear attacking after the shot. Bullets should weigh at least 165 grains.

Black Bear Range

Signs of Bear Activity

DAMAGED TREES or bushes are common feeding signs. A bear rips down a branch with its claws, then strips off the fruit or berries.

TRACKS have distinct claw marks and measure 3½ to 5 inches wide. The front foot is 4 to 5 inches long; the hind foot 6 to 7 inches.

DROPPINGS reveal what bear have been eating. They often contain berries, grass, hair, and wood eaten along with insects.

Bear Hunting Techniques

BAIT black bear with bags of meat scraps. Hang the bags above ground so the scent spreads. Bait several different locations before the season, then select a stand near a bait-site that bear visit regularly.

FOLLOW hounds on foot or horseback until they tree or corner a bear. Hunters scout a potential area to locate fresh tracks, then release the dogs. Even if the scent is cold, good dogs will pick up the bear's trail.

Small Game

The nation's hunters spend more time in pursuit of small game than on any other type of hunting. The sport's popularity stems from the relative ease of finding game. With a little scouting, you can probably locate small game within a few miles of your home. Even with a minimum of equipment, you can bring home a tasty meal.

In this book, the term small game includes only the small mammals commonly hunted for sport and food, namely rabbit, hare, squirrel and raccoon.

Even the novice has a reasonable chance to bag rabbits or squirrels. But this does not mean that small game hunting is easy. Your success will improve as your level of skill increases. And you can apply the skills you gain to other types of hunting.

Small game hunters have ample opportunity to enjoy their sport. Most hunting seasons last at least six months, and some are continuous. Because you can

find these animals close to home, you can make frequent short trips, which is difficult when hunting most other types of game. Almost all states and provinces have liberal bag limits.

Most hunters use shotguns or .22 caliber rimfire rifles. But some prefer a combination gun with a .22 caliber rifle barrel on top and a 20 gauge shotgun barrel on the bottom. Combination guns are ideal for small game because you can fire one barrel at standing animals and the other at running targets. Hunters also use small-caliber centerfire rifles, muz-zleloading rifles and shotguns, and bows with blunt-tipped arrows.

A pair of waterproof leather boots is a good invest-ment. With the possible exceptions of brush pants, a burr-proof jacket with a game pouch, binoculars, and a small knife for field dressing, you need little other equipment.

Many hunters compare rabbit and squirrel meat to chicken. Raccoon tends to be oily and has a distinc-tive flavor of its own. Small game tastes better if you remove the entrails soon after killing the animal.

Cottontail Rabbits

Each year, hunters throughout the United States bag 30 to 40 million cottontail rabbits. This staggering total results from the cottontail's tremendous reproductive rate, and its ability to adapt to a wide range of habitats and foods.

Cottontails breed in the spring and summer, producing up to eight litters, each with three to six young. They prefer brushy edges and woodlots, but can live almost anywhere with the exception of dense forests. They eat practically any type of green plant. When green vegetation dies back, they switch to twigs and bark.

Rabbits start feeding before dawn and continue for two or three hours. They resume feeding at sunset. They move about most on calm, sunny days. Rain or wind drives them into heavy cover.

A cottontail spends most of the day sitting in a *form,* a shallow depression in grass or snow. The grass eventually wears away, or the snow melts down and compacts. Often a form is concealed by overhanging grass or other type of overhead cover.

Rabbits use their superb hearing to sense impending danger. To escape, they bolt away on established travel lanes. Cottontails run in an elusive, zig-zag pattern, but their speed is not as fast as many hunters believe. They normally run 12 to 15 miles-per-hour, but can reach 20.

Normally, cottontails will not run far. They spend their entire lives within a few acres, getting to know every feature of that area. Rather than run straight away, a rabbit will circle so it can stay in familiar territory. When frightened, it will often slip into a woodchuck burrow or brush pile.

You can bag some cottontails by walking through likely cover, looking for rabbits in their forms. Upland bird hunters frequently flush rabbits by moving in typical walk-and-wait fashion. Like most game animals, a cottontail becomes nervous when a nearby hunter stands motionless, and will often bound from its resting spot.

Hunting with dogs offers an interesting and effective alternative. Most hunters use slow-moving hounds, like beagles and bassets. When the dogs get close, the rabbit begins moving in a large circle and will eventually pass within shooting range of the hunter. Almost any dog will chase cottontails, but if it works too fast, the rabbit will dash under a brush pile or down a hole.

Rabbits may contract a bacterial disease called *tularemia,* which causes them to behave listlessly and eventually kills them. But the disease is rare. One researcher found it in only 2 of 12,000 rabbits he examined. Nevertheless, refrain from shooting rabbits that move slowly or otherwise behave unusually. Tularemia can be transmitted to humans who eat or handle the flesh of infected animals.

Cottontail Rabbit Range

To hit zig-zagging cottontails, most hunters use shotguns with modified or improved cylinder chokes, and No. 6 shot. But when rabbits are in their forms or feeding in the open, a .22 rifle with a scope may enable you to get a shot before they spook.

Where to Find Cottontails

STRIP COVER, like brushy fence-lines and hedgerows, makes ideal cottontail habitat. The brush and high grass provide food and cover.

ABANDONED FARMS offer a variety of hiding spots. Look for rabbits around groves, under old machinery, or in tall grass or brush.

BRUSH PILES provide good escape cover. A fox or owl would have little chance of reaching a rabbit beneath the logs and sticks.

COTTONTAILS are named for their fluffy white tail. The fur on the upper part of the body is grayish-brown with black tips. The undersides are white. Adults measure 14 to 19 inches long and weigh 2½ to 3½ pounds.

Signs of Cottontail Activity

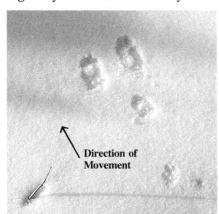

Direction of Movement

TRACKS of cottontails have side-by-side hind prints ahead of smaller front prints. One front foot falls ahead of the other.

RUNWAYS in tall grass serve as escape routes. Rabbits usually follow the same paths through cover, eventually matting down the vegetation.

FEEDING SIGNS include girdled shrubs or saplings, and cleanly-snipped twigs. Cottontails prefer the bark of sumac (above) and fruit trees.

How to Hunt With Hounds

RELEASE the dogs where you find plenty of sign. Beagles have excellent noses and will scour the ground thoroughly to find fresh scent. They will methodically follow the trail, slowly pushing the rabbit ahead.

WAIT in the area where the dogs first detect fresh scent. A rabbit will usually circle and return to the spot where it was flushed. If it does not circle, try to predict its escape route, then attempt to intercept it.

Other Cottontail Hunting Techniques

LOCATE a form with fresh sign. Droppings are round and about ⅜-inch across. A rabbit will seldom move far from its form.

WALK around the form in ever-widening circles. Look for the rabbit in clumps of brush, around the bases of trees, in tall grass, or in any dense cover. Continue walking until you cover the entire area within a 100-foot radius of the cottontail's form. Follow any fresh tracks you encounter.

WATCH for rabbit tracks as you walk a strip of cover like a brushy fenceline. A retriever or flushing dog will scare up tight-holding rabbits.

HUNT around abandoned farmsteads. Look for rabbits as you round the corner of a building and be ready for a quick shot.

FLUSH cottontails by beating a brush pile with a stick. Or climb on top of the brush pile, jump up and down, and yell to scare out rabbits.

Snowshoe Hares

The *snowshoe* is named for its oversized hind feet, which provide a large surface area to support the animal on soft snow.

Noted for their dramatic cycles of abundance, snowshoe populations have been known to peak at 3400 animals per square mile. Following a peak year, the population often declines to such a low level that hunters have difficulty finding enough animals to hunt. A complete cycle takes about 10 years.

Snowshoes behave much like cottontails and eat similar foods. But they are more likely to feed at night. They prefer conifer swamps and young hardwood forests rather than brushy edges. Snowshoes are larger, faster and better jumpers.

Hunting with hounds works as well for showshoes as it does for cottontails. Most hunters use beagles, but a breed with longer legs will have less trouble pushing through deep snow. Like cottontails, snowshoes will stay ahead of a dog and circle back toward a waiting hunter.

Snowshoe hunters generally use shotguns with improved cylinder or modified chokes, and No. 4 to 6 shot. A snowshoe can run up to 30 miles-per-hour and change direction in the middle of a leap, so a tight choke is less effective. To increase their shooting range, many still-hunters use .22 rifles

Snowshoe Hare Range

SNOWSHOES, also called *varying hares,* vary in color depending on the season. The coat is white in winter and brown in summer (inset). Snowshoes are 16 to 21 inches long and weigh 3 to 4 pounds.

LOOK for a snowshoe's black eye and black-tipped ears when hunting in snow. You can spot the animals more easily after a mid-winter thaw, because their white bodies stand out against bare ground.

FOLLOW tracks after a fresh snowfall. About 2 inches of new snow over a hard crust makes for ideal tracking. If the snow is more than a foot deep, a pair of snowshoes will make walking much easier.

Gray Squirrels

A gray squirrel leaping through the treetops will test the marksmanship of any hunter. Using their wide-angle vision and sharp hearing, squirrels quickly detect a hunter, then scurry away before he can shoot.

To avoid being seen, a squirrel moves to the opposite side of a tree trunk or limb. Or it flattens its body against the tree. Once the hunter has walked past, it scampers to its den and stays there until it feels safe.

Good habitat will produce one gray squirrel per acre. Thus, a square mile of prime woodlands could hold over 600 squirrels. How plentiful gray squirrels are in a given year depends mainly on the previous year's acorn crop. Other foods include walnuts, hickory nuts, pecans, berries and corn.

Gray squirrels begin feeding just before sunrise. They continue for two or three hours, then retire to their dens. They resume feeding in late afternoon and may remain active until just after sunset. Squirrels move about most on calm, sunny days. Cold or windy weather keeps them denned up. They seldom travel more than 300 yards from their dens.

Gray Squirrel Range

Mature deciduous forests throughout the eastern United States hold gray squirrels. They favor mixed hardwoods with an abundance of mature oaks, dense undergrowth and few open areas.

GRAY SQUIRRELS have a grayish back and sides, and whitish or brownish undersides. A solid black color phase predominates in some areas. Adults measure 14 to 21 inches from head to tail and weigh ¾ to 1½ pounds.

Signs of Squirrel Activity

ACORN SHELLS at the base of a tree indicate a squirrel den somewhere above. Sign in a large forest is usually left by grays.

STRIPPED CORNCOBS also reveal squirrel activity. Sign along a fenceline or in a small woodlot is generally that of fox squirrels.

HOLES in the snow with leaves and debris around the edge are made by squirrels digging up food caches. Tracks often have clear toe marks.

Fox Squirrels

Named for its reddish, fox-colored fur, the fox squirrel differs from the gray squirrel in behavior and habitat. Some hunters maintain that it is less wary and easier to outwit than the gray.

Fox squirrels spend more time on the ground than grays and rely less on treetops as escape routes. When threatened, they run straight for their dens or hide behind trunks or limbs. Unlike grays, they seldom feed in early morning. They are more active during midday and stray farther from their dens. Fox squirrels can often be seen lying on a limb basking in the sun.

Many hunters refer to fox squirrels as red squirrels. But the true red squirrel is much smaller and is not considered a game animal.

Fox squirrels prefer woodlots, farm groves and strips of timber rather than forests. Like grays, they eat acorns and other nuts. In agricultural areas, corn and other crops make up a high percentage of the diet. Squirrels get most of their water from their food.

Fox Squirrel Range

Both gray and fox squirrels make a variety of calls. A series of rapid *cherks,* or barks, serves as a warning signal to other squirrels. The familiar chatter means squirrels are approaching one another. A low-pitched chuckle signifies contentment.

FOX SQUIRRELS are dull orange on the underside, the tips of the ears and the top of the tail. Some varieties are black or gray. Adults measure 19 to 29 inches from head to tail and weigh 1 to 2¾ pounds.

DENS are made by squirrels gnawing at small openings like woodpecker holes. Dens are about 4 inches wide and at least 10 feet off the ground.

HICKORY TREES produce nuts which draw squirrels. You can easily identify hickories in early fall; they turn yellow earlier than other trees.

NESTS consist of twigs and leaves piled into a crotch or woven into the branches. Nests are 1 to 2 feet across, and 20 feet or more above ground.

101

HIDING on the opposite side of a tree trunk is the squirrel's favorite method of eluding the hunter. No matter where the hunter is, the squirrel will always be on the other side of the tree.

Hunting for Squirrels

You can tell when to go squirrel hunting by watching the animals in your yard or a local park. When these squirrels begin feeding and moving about, so will their wild counterparts.

Squirrel hunting is best in early fall, when the animals are gathering and burying nuts. Windy days make for poor hunting. Squirrels seldom move about when the wind exceeds 15 miles-per-hour. Hunting success picks up dramatically after a period of windy, rainy or snowy weather.

Another good time to hunt is during the major breeding period, which starts in December or January. Squirrels lose their normal caution as they begin courtship. Sometimes a half-dozen or more animals fearlessly chase each other through the trees, paying little attention to hunters.

If the ground is dry, you can locate more squirrels with your ears than with your eyes. Listen carefully for squirrels scampering across limbs or over fallen leaves, or for barking and chattering.

To stand-hunt for squirrels, choose a comfortable spot at the base of a tree. Your stand should overlook an area that shows signs of squirrel activity. Then wait for the animals to appear. Study each tree, looking for tufts of orange or gray fur, the flick of a tail, or a suspicious bump which could be a squirrel's head.

When still-hunting for squirrels, walk slowly and quietly through an area with many nests and dens. As a general rule, walk no more than 100 yards in 15 minutes. Stop periodically to watch the treetops and listen for movement. If you scare a squirrel into its den, sit down and be patient. It will usually come back out in 15 to 20 minutes.

If you shoot a squirrel, do not pick it up immediately. The sight of a hunter spooks squirrels longer than the sound of a shot. If you do not move, they will resume feeding in 5 to 10 minutes.

Most squirrel hunters use .22 rifles with scopes up to 4x, 20 gauge shotguns with No. 6 shot, or .22-20 gauge combination guns.

How to Stand-hunt for Squirrels

SIT quietly, glassing trees with binoculars. Choose a spot with the sun at your back. That way, you can see squirrels but they may not see you.

CALL to coax squirrels into revealing themselves. Calls include (1) a blow call and (2) a bellows call. Either can be used to produce barks and chatters.

CLICK quarters together to imitate a scolding squirrel. Place one coin slightly lower than the other and rapidly snap the lower coin.

Other Squirrel Hunting Techniques

TEAM-HUNT with a companion. With this method, squirrels cannot hide on the opposite side of a tree without being seen. Be ready to shoot the moment a squirrel moves to your side of the tree.

TOSS a stick or rock to the opposite side of a tree. Or tie a string to a bush on one side of the tree, then move to the other side and tug it sharply. The motion will frighten squirrels to your side.

FLOAT-HUNT along streams bordered by nut trees. The extra sunlight and moisture result in good nut crops that attract squirrels.

FOLLOW your dog until it trees a squirrel. Then try to maneuver into position for a shot. A barking dog may scare the squirrel to your side.

103

Raccoon

Many people think of raccoon as mischievous, playful animals. But in reality, adult raccoon are ferocious fighters. They have needle-sharp teeth and can kill or maim hunting dogs twice their size.

Hardwood forests near water make good raccoon habitat. They also live in marshy lowlands, and can adapt to habitats ranging from the Florida mangroves to the arid plains of New Mexico.

Raccoon eat almost any kind of food including berries, fruits, nuts, frogs, crayfish and insects. Sweet corn is a favorite. They hold their food with small, nimble paws that closely resemble human hands.

An adult raccoon may travel up to 5 miles on its nightly feeding rounds, especially in warm weather. During the day, they often den up in hollow trees. But they may bed in the tall vegetation along the edge of a marsh, in a culvert, or in the ground burrow of another animal. Raccoon frequently use different dens or beds on successive days. They den up for a period after heavy snow; in cold climates they may hibernate.

Ranked among the most intelligent game animals, raccoon also have excellent hearing and good eyesight. They can run up to 15 miles-per-hour and are good swimmers.

The vast majority of raccoon hunting is done with hounds, especially Walkers, black-and-tans and redbones. Tracking is easiest on damp, cool nights with a slight breeze. Some dogs can pick up a cold trail, making it possible to hunt in daylight.

When pursued by hounds, raccoon usually run in large circles, crawling in and out of holes and climbing up and down trees to lose the dogs. They may jump to the ground from as high as 50 feet and scurry away unharmed. They will stay in a tree only when the hounds get so close that other avenues of escape are impossible.

Early in the season you may be able to call raccoon. After dark, take a stand along a streambank, lakeshore, or cornfield. Use tapes, records or calls to imitate an injured bird or rabbit.

The majority of raccoon hunters use .22 rifles, although some prefer 20 gauge shotguns with No. 6 or 7½ shot. Where legal, a few hunters use small-caliber pistols.

Raccoon Range

RACCOON have a black, mask-like band across the eyes and black rings on the tail. Most raccoon weigh between 15 and 20 pounds. The largest on record, 62 pounds, 6 ounces, was shot in Wisconsin in 1950.

Where to Find Raccoon

LOOK for holes in trees that could be den sites. You will seldom see raccoon during the day, but an area with many dens would be a good spot to hunt after dark.

CHECK for tracks in the soft dirt around ponds, marshes or streams. Raccoon go to water to drink and to find foods like crayfish, frogs and small fish.

How to Hunt With Hounds

RELEASE the hounds and allow them to range ahead to pick up raccoon scent. To better control the hounds, some hunters keep them on leash until the dogs detect fresh scent, then turn them loose.

LISTEN for the hounds to start baying, then follow the sound. Some hunters use orange or red headlamps to find their way through the woods. The colored light is less noticeable to a raccoon than a white light.

CONTINUE to follow the dogs until they either tree the raccoon or lose it. Sometimes the chase goes on for miles. Hunters can tell when their dogs tree a raccoon, because the baying becomes more intense.

Upland Game Birds

A big rooster pheasant bursting from cover would appear to be an easy target. But as every upland bird hunter knows, an unexpected flush will test the skill and composure of even the best wingshooter.

The term *upland* means high ground. But upland birds can also be found in and around lowlands. Pheasants frequent marsh edges and sharp-tailed grouse often live in bogs. Migratory upland birds also congregate in lowland areas. Woodcock feed along moist streambanks and mourning doves gather near water holes.

All upland birds have keen eyesight and sharp hearing. They have a poorly-developed sense of smell, if they can detect odors at all. It pays to approach upland birds quietly and inconspicuously.

The meat of upland game birds varies greatly in color and flavor. The dark breast meat of woodcock and sharptails is laced with blood vessels that supply the muscles with oxygen, enabling the birds to fly long distances. Birds with white breast meat, like ruffed grouse and wild turkey, have fewer blood vessels and cannot fly as far.

Upland bird hunters need little equipment other than waterproof boots and a thorn-proof jacket and pants. If hunting in dense woods or brush, you may need protective glasses.

With the exception of the small-caliber rifles used for wild turkey, upland bird hunters almost always use shotguns. The choke and shot size varies with the size of the bird and the usual shooting distance.

Ring-necked Pheasants

Every pheasant hunter has been mystified upon arriving at the spot where he saw a rooster land, only to find no trace of the bird.

This Chinese import deserves its reputation as one of the most wily and elusive upland game birds. Its first instinct is to run rather than fly. And despite its large size and gaudy colors, a rooster can slink away unnoticed in ankle-high cover. Sometimes a bird will sit tight, refusing to budge unless you actually step on it.

Pheasants rely on excellent eyesight and good hearing to elude hunters. They can detect ground vibrations not recognizable to humans. These vibrations often cause roosters to crow.

Ringnecks thrive in fertile agricultural areas with good nesting and wintering cover. In spring, they nest in moderately dense cover like hay meadows, clover fields and roadside ditches. They continue to use these areas as roosting sites into the fall, but also roost in weedy cropfields, short slough grass, willow patches and woodlots. They occasionally roost in trees. Pheasants need heavier cover to escape winter storms.

Primary foods include grain crops like corn, wheat, milo and soybeans. They also eat weed seeds and insects. The birds pick up grit in fields and along roads. This helps their gizzard to grind food.

From June through August, hen pheasants remain with their broods of four to eight chicks. By fall, the chicks begin to mature and the groups break up. As winter approaches, pheasants often flock together where they can find food and heavy cover. Flocks may contain hundreds of birds.

Despite the fact that pheasants are among the hardiest of game birds, their average life-span is only nine months. Normally, only 30 percent of the birds survive from one year to the next, even where there is no hunting season.

In most states and provinces, only roosters are legal game. Pheasants are *polygamous,* meaning that one rooster can mate with many hens. Research has proven that hunters can harvest up to 90 percent of the roosters without affecting the next year's hatch.

Hunters can quickly distinguish the colorful rooster from the drab hen. In addition, roosters often cackle on take-off, removing any doubt about the bird's sex. The typical rooster measures 30 to 36 inches from head to tail and weighs 2½ to 3 pounds. The hen has a much shorter tail and weighs about one-half pound less.

Roosters have spurs on the lower part of the leg. The spurs grow longer and sharper as the bird gets older, reaching ¾-inch on three-year-old birds. They use their spurs in spring territorial battles. The sharp spurs on an old rooster can badly scratch a hunter or a dog.

When a rooster bursts from cover, it quickly reaches a speed of 35 to 40 miles-per-hour. It may fly up to one mile, but usually only a few hundred yards. A bird generally spends its entire life in an area of one-half square mile or less, leaving that area only if food or cover becomes inadequate.

Ring-necked Pheasant Range

Typical Pheasant Habitat

FERTILE CROPLANDS offer a good food supply. But expanses of corn and other row crops with little cover support few pheasants.

NESTING COVER is vital to pheasants. Hens need grassy cover at least 12 inches high which remains unmowed until after nesting.

WINTER COVER includes cattail sloughs, thick brush or willows, and woodlots. With good cover, pheasants can survive to −50°F.

RINGNECKS get their name from the white ring around the rooster's neck. Both sexes have brownish tails with black crossbars. The rooster has a reddish-copper breast and a powder-blue rump. Its head has shades of metallic blue, green and purple with a bright red eye patch. The hen (inset) is tan with dark flecks and creamy mottling.

PHEASANT LOCATIONS change as the day progresses. In early morning, look for ringnecks in roosting areas like (1) roadside ditches and (2) drainage ditches with grassy cover, and (3) woodlots. By mid-morning, most birds begin feeding in (4) corn and (5) soybean fields. In early afternoon, look for them in loafing cover like (6) light grass around the edge of a cornfield. In late afternoon, they return to roosting sites.

Pheasant Hunting Strategies

The pheasant hunting season can be split into two parts: the first few days and the rest of the season. Young pheasants lack the wariness of birds hatched the previous year, so the early days of the season usually offer the easiest hunting. But once the easier birds are gone, you will find it much more difficult to outwit the remaining roosters.

EARLY SEASON. You can locate a good area before the season opens by driving through the countryside and looking for pheasants. The best time to spot the birds is around sunrise on a clear, calm day with dew on the grass. You may also see pheasants in late afternoon. Another way to locate a good hunting area is to look for abundant nesting cover. Chances are there will be birds in the vicinity. If you find a promising location, ask the farmer if you can return to hunt once the season begins.

Early-season hunters often find most of the land covered with crops. In this situation, pheasants may be almost anywhere. To flush birds from large crop or stubble fields, hunters conduct drives. With this much cover still standing, other techniques may not be as productive.

Ringnecks usually flush close in early season, so a shotgun with an improved cylinder or modified choke works best. Use shot no larger than No. 6.

LATE SEASON. Once farmers harvest their crops, the birds have fewer places to hide. But birds that survive to late season have learned to evade danger and will often flush far ahead of approaching hunters. Or they will hold extremely tight and let hunters walk past.

In late season, roosters hole up in much heavier cover than they did earlier in the year. They prefer areas with tall trees or other cover that will break the wind. Look for them in brushy woodlots, thick fencelines, and drainage ditches lined with slough grass. A favorite hiding spot is a fringe of cattails around the edge of a shallow wetland. Although it prefers heavy cover, a late-season rooster will sometimes seek refuge in a patch of grass not much larger than his body. After a snowfall, hunters often find pheasants under clumps of grass covered with snow. The birds evidently allow themselves to become snowed in.

To bag late-season roosters, one hunter blocks a possible escape route while another approaches from the opposite end of cover. If a rooster flushes too far ahead of the walking hunter, the blocker may get a shot.

For long-range shooting in late season, use a modified or full choke shotgun with No. 4 to 6 shot.

PLAN your strategy carefully before you begin your hunt. Try to identify a route that will take you through the best cover and lead you back to your vehicle with a minimum of back-tracking.

LOOK for early-season ringnecks scattered throughout cropfields, along grassy field edges and in brush patches (above). In late season the birds concentrate in heavy cover like brush patches and farm groves (below).

110

Hunting Pheasants With a Dog

Statistics show that hunters who use dogs bag twice as many ringnecks as those who do not. Most hunters agree that flushers and retrievers work best in heavy cover. Preferred breeds include springer spaniels and Labrador retrievers. Some hunters prefer pointing dogs for large expanses of light, grassy cover, but a wily rooster will often run rather than hold to a point.

A dog with good retrieving skills will seldom lose a crippled ringneck. Pheasants are notoriously difficult to kill. A wounded rooster will usually run off and burrow under heavy grass or brush, where a hunter without a dog would have practically no chance of finding it. A good dog will mark the bird down and relentlessly pursue it through even the thickest tangle of vegetation.

Skilled handlers refuse to work their dogs in standing cornfields or fields of other tall row crops. To a ringneck, an open row is an invitation to run. And most dogs will follow, often disappearing into the field and flushing birds at the opposite end.

A novice pheasant hunter tends to over-command his dog, continually directing it to hunt likely-looking spots. Instead, let the dog use its nose to decide where to hunt. Allow it to range back and forth across cover until it finds fresh scent.

HUNT strip-cover with your dog on the downwind side. When the dog detects fresh scent, it will move into the cover and flush or point the bird. Late in the season, another hunter should post at the end of the strip.

FOLLOW your dog through a large expanse of cover. A flushing dog may run when it picks up a scent. You must keep up so birds do not flush out of range. With pointing breeds, you do not have to stay as close.

SEND your dog into a thick patch of cover to save you time and energy. Keep track of its location by watching and listening for moving grass or brush. Or attach a bell to the dog's collar.

Hunting Alone for Pheasants

A ringneck's inclination to run rather than fly makes it one of the most difficult birds to hunt by yourself. But you can greatly improve your odds by choosing the right type of spot and by using proven, one-hunter techniques.

You are most likely to flush pheasants from small, isolated pieces of cover, such as a patch of short slough grass surrounded by a plowed field. In a large block of heavy cover, a rooster can easily give you the slip.

If you walk steadily in a straight line, pheasants will probably sit tight and let you pass. But if you follow a zig-zag path, walking a few steps, then stopping for a moment, nearby pheasants generally become nervous and fly.

Watch and listen carefully for any indication of pheasant movement. If the cover is not too thick, you might catch a glimpse of a rooster running ahead. On a still day, you may hear the slight rustling of a rooster sneaking through the grass.

SELECT manageable-sized pieces of cover when hunting alone. Try to push the birds toward a spot where the cover suddenly ends. Pheasants are reluctant to run into an open field and will usually flush near the edge.

RUSH a clump of cover that you suspect holds a ringneck. To prevent the bird from running out before you get there, sneak as close as possible before rushing. The element of surprise usually causes the bird to flush.

HUNT the sunny side of cover on frosty mornings. Pheasants move to the sunlit side to warm up and dry any moisture on their feathers. Later in the day, the birds may retreat deeper into the cover.

FOLLOW fresh tracks in the snow. Rooster tracks are slightly larger and farther apart than those of a hen. Often the tracks will end at a snow-covered clump of grass. You may have to kick the clump to flush the bird.

Driving for Pheasants

Driving takes advantage of the ringneck's habit of running at the sight or sound of humans. A row of hunters moves through all or part of a large block of cover, while posters wait quietly at the end.

Drivers may flush some pheasants, but more often the birds run to the end of the field. When the drivers approach the posters, the birds realize they are trapped and explode from cover.

If the field is too wide to cover in one pass, the posters can take a vehicle to the end they are blocking. The drivers can take the vehicle back to the opposite end, then make another drive. Or the posters can return, while the drivers start another pass from the end where they finished.

When driving cover that narrows toward one end, start from the widest end. This way you will push the birds into a smaller area, increasing the likelihood of someone getting a shot.

DRIVE pheasants from the heaviest cover to the lightest. Pushing birds into sparse vegetation forces them to fly. If you drive from light to heavy cover, the birds are more likely to find a safe hiding spot.

AVOID driving into the sun, especially when it is low in the sky. The glare may blind you or prevent you from distinguishing a rooster from a hen. If you must hunt into the sun, listen for a cackle or look for a long tail.

General Pheasant Hunting Tips

CHOOSE *dirty* cropfields when hunting ringnecks. The weeds provide cover and food that is lacking in clean, well-manicured fields.

LEAPFROG stretches of cover. Drop off a partner, drive ahead, then start walking. He walks to the car, drives ahead of you, then resumes walking.

LOOK for the tallest, thickest cover, especially in cold or windy weather. Trees or tall weeds offer better shelter than the surrounding lower cover.

Bobwhite Quail

A covey of bobwhites exploding from cover can rattle even the veteran hunter. Often, each bird flies in a different direction. In the confusion, the hunter may shoot hurriedly without touching a feather.

Despite their stubby wings, quail can fly up to 30 miles-per-hour and change direction instantly as they dodge through cover. But they usually fly less than 200 yards. Bobwhites are also excellent runners; in fact, they seldom fly unless threatened.

When alarmed, a member of the covey emits a barely audible signal which tells the others to freeze. They squat and remain motionless, relying on camouflage to conceal themselves until the threat passes. If they feel too conspicuous, they scurry to another hiding spot.

Cocks have a white throat patch and a white line through the eye. On hens, the throat patch and line are buff-colored. Bobwhites measure about 10 inches long and weigh 6 to 8 ounces.

Unlike pheasants, bobwhites are *monogamous*, meaning that a cock breeds with only one hen. Quail eggs hatch from May to early July. The cock helps incubate the eggs and raise the chicks. By the start of hunting season, the chicks resemble the adults and the covey consists of 10 to 15 birds.

The birds thrive in areas with a mixture of grasslands, woodlands and brush adjacent to croplands. They use grasslands mainly for nesting; woodlands and brush provide roosting and escape cover. Bobwhites cannot survive in a climate with prolonged periods of deep snow or severe cold. They are unable to dig through deep snow to find food, and their small bodies will not retain enough heat.

Nearly all bobwhites live within 50 to 100 feet of field borders. Seldom will they be found in the middle of a cropfield or woods.

The bobwhite's diet consists mainly of weed seeds, but they also eat insects, acorns and crops like corn, soybeans, wheat and milo. On hot, clear days, the birds feed in early morning and late afternoon. In midday, they take periodic dust baths along sunny field edges. But during cool, damp weather, bobwhites often stay in their roosts until mid-morning, feed intermittently until dark, then return to their roosts.

Each year, predators, severe weather and hunting take a heavy toll on the bobwhite population. On the average, a bird lives about 8½ months; only 15 to 20 percent survive to the next breeding season.

Bobwhite Quail Range

Where to Find Bobwhite Quail

LOOK for bobwhite quail in an area that offers ample food and good roosting, escape and nesting cover. The birds feed in (1) harvested cropfields and along (2) weedy field borders. They find roosting and escape cover along (3) wooded stream courses, (4) woodlot edges, (5) grassy drainage ditches, (6) brushy fencelines and in (7) tall weeds around abandoned buildings. They nest in (8) fields of sedge grass and (9) old pastures.

114

BOBWHITE QUAIL roost on the ground. During cool weather, they form a *roosting ring,* huddling in a plate-sized circle with their tails pointing toward the center. This tactic preserves body heat. Bobwhites prefer a roost-ing site with plenty of open space above them, enabling them to flush quickly should the need arise. Roosts gener-ally have a south or west exposure, so the ground stays warm in late afternoon.

OSAGE ORANGE means good quail cover. Its sharp spines prevent cattle from eating the underbrush. Look for the large, yellow fruits.

GIANT RAGWEED provides roost-ing and escape cover. The plants stand up to 12 feet tall. Ragweed seeds may be a major source of food in fall.

LESPEDEZA, or Japan Clover, pro-duces seeds which quail eat in winter. Found mainly in the South, it is planted for erosion control.

Hunting for Bobwhite Quail

To many bobwhite hunters, the biggest thrill comes from watching good pointing dogs in action.

A lone hunter who works the cover slowly and thoroughly can kick up some bobwhites by himself. But if the birds decide to hold tight, hunting can be extremely difficult without a dog.

Most hunters prefer English pointers or English setters for large expanses of cover. Brittanys and German shorthairs also work well, but do not cover quite as much ground. Handlers allow the dogs to range far ahead of the hunting party. When a dog detects fresh scent, it locks on point. The covey freezes, giving the hunters plenty of time to move into position.

Most of the birds burst from cover in unison. After the initial flush, work the area a little longer because a straggler or two may remain. Flushing the last birds is often more difficult.

Quail usually fly only a short distance, so you can flush them again. Sometimes the covey stays together, sometimes it breaks up. Watch carefully because the birds may veer off to the side just before they land.

Early season offers the best bobwhite hunting. Coveys consist mainly of young birds that have never been hunted. But as the season progresses, quail become much more unpredictable. Some birds will flush when you slam your car door. Others will run rather than hold to a point. Flushed birds will fly two or three times farther than they did in early season.

Finding downed quail can be difficult, even with a good dog. Some hunters maintain that the scent *washes off* as the birds fly. On the ground, bobwhites compress their feathers so little scent can escape. Bird dogs may walk within inches of wounded quail without finding them. Because of their small size and excellent camouflage, quail can hide in the lightest cover.

Many quail hunters prefer 20 gauge, double-barreled shotguns with improved cylinder and modified chokes. Small shot, usually No. 7½ or 8, works best.

Bobwhite Hunting Basics

FLUSH a covey by walking toward the birds. Spread apart to increase the chances of getting a shot and to prevent shooting toward each other.

PICK a single bird and concentrate on that shot. Resist the tendency to *flock shoot*. A wild shot at the covey rarely brings down a bird.

LEARN to judge your effective shooting distance. Because bobwhites are so small, they are probably closer than you think.

Other Quail Hunting Techniques

FOLLOW your pointing dogs using a 4-wheel drive vehicle or a mule-drawn quail wagon, or on horseback. This technique enables you to cover more territory than you could on foot.

HUNT for bobwhites by yourself using the walk-and-wait technique (page 61). Avoid large blocks of cover. Instead, work brush piles, field corners, narrow strips, or other small areas where the birds are easier to find.

Tips for Hunting Bobwhites

LISTEN for the typical *bob-bob-white* whistle during the mating period. You will find birds in the same area once the hunting season opens.

LOOK for a circle of droppings to pinpoint bobwhite roosting sites. The birds often roost in the same spot for several consecutive nights.

CARRY a snakebite kit when hunting in snake country. The kit can be used on dogs as well as humans. Some hunters also wear protective leggings.

California Quail

California quail, also called *valley quail*, prefer semi-arid desert brushlands. They feed on the seeds of weeds and brush, and roost in dense patches of tall shrubs or low trees. The birds need water each day and are seldom far from streams, springs or water holes.

In fall, they form large packs numbering from 50 to over 100 birds. They prefer to run rather than fly. When flushed, they usually go only a short distance, then land in bushes or trees.

A good pointing dog can pin down an entire pack by circling the birds. If they fly, watch where they land. They hold tighter on the second flush.

Ideal shotguns for the quail on these pages are 12 or 20 gauge double barrels with modified and improved cylinder chokes. These guns give you an open pattern for birds that hold and a tight pattern for those that flush at long range. Most hunters use No. 7½ shot.

California Quail Range

CALIFORNIA QUAIL have a scaled breast, grayish-brown flanks with white streaks, and a teardrop-shaped plume. Males (above) have a black throat with a white border, and a chestnut patch on the belly. Females are less boldly marked. California quail weigh 6 to 7 ounces.

Gambel's Quail

Sometimes called *desert quail,* Gambel's quail are usually found along brushy slopes and in river valleys of arid and semi-arid deserts. They roost in dense thickets or trees, and feed on the seeds of weeds and brush. Normally the birds get enough water from their foods and the dew. But during dry conditions, they rely on a watering site.

The birds come out to feed early and late. They spend the rest of the day in brushy cover to escape the heat. In cool weather, they leave their roosts earlier and may remain in the open all day.

If you approach Gambel's quail in the open, they will probably run before you can get a shot. But if you wait until they move to cover, the birds are more likely to hold. A good pointing dog will improve your odds.

Gambel's Quail Range

Poisonous snakes are rarely a problem, but you should bring a snakebite kit to be safe. Some hunters also wear leather or plastic leggings.

GAMBEL'S QUAIL resemble California quail, but their buff-white belly is not scaled, and the cap and flanks on the male (above) are reddish-brown. Males also have a black patch on the lower part of the breast. Gambel's quail weigh 5½ to 6½ ounces.

Mountain Quail

Few upland game birds are as difficult to hunt as mountain quail. They will run at the sight of a hunter and even a good pointing dog has difficulty pinning them down.

Found at elevations of 2000 to 10,000 feet, mountain quail live along brushy edges of conifer forests or along brush-lined streams. They eat berries, clover, wild oats, and seeds of weeds and grasses; the birds roost under heavy brush or in small conifers. They roam over large areas, retreating to lower elevations in late fall to avoid severe weather.

Coveys generally number only seven to nine birds. They do not form packs, but hunters sometimes see loose groups of birds feeding in the same area.

A flusher or retriever is usually more thorough than a pointing dog and more likely to find single birds that sit tight. Field boots will prevent your dog from injuring its feet on sharp rocks and cactus spines.

Mountain Quail Range

MOUNTAIN QUAIL have a grayish-brown back, a chestnut throat, and chestnut flank with heavy white bars. The head and breast are bluish-gray. Two long, dark feathers form the plume. The sexes look alike. Mountain quail weigh 8 to 9 ounces.

Scaled Quail

Some hunters refer to scaled quail as *blue quail;* others call them *blue racers.* These birds are even more likely to run than mountain quail.

Scaled quail live in semi-arid desert grasslands and in grassy brushlands. They prefer weed and brush seeds for food. The birds roost in dense clumps of brush, grass or weeds. Their water requirements are similar to those of Gambel's quail. In some states, conservation agencies have installed watering devices, helping both quail species to survive during dry periods.

Hunters debate the value of a dog. Some maintain that dogs will flush scaled quail too far ahead, and that they are not needed to find downed birds on the open ground.

If you spot a covey, rush the birds to startle them into flying. Even if you are out of range, shoot to scatter the birds and scare up stragglers. Then hunt the singles, because they will be more likely to hold.

Scaled Quail Range

SCALED QUAIL have breast feathers with dark margins, giving them a scaled appearance. The breast is bluish-gray; the head grayish-brown with a distinctive white-tipped crest. The crest is larger on males (above). Scaled quail weigh 6 to 7 ounces.

RUFFED GROUSE have a broad, black or dark brown band on the tail. The band is unbroken on most males (above), but broken on the center two feathers on females. There are two color phases, red and gray. Red- phase birds are more common in the South and at low altitudes; grays (inset) predominate in the North and at high altitudes. Grouse measure 17 to 20 inches long. They weigh 16 to 24 ounces, but occasionally reach 2 pounds.

Ruffed Grouse

Some hunters maintain that a ruffed grouse will intentionally select a flight path that places a tree directly in the line of fire. Whether intentional or not, the ruffed grouse is a difficult target for even the best wingshooters.

Grouse accelerate rapidly, reaching a speed of 40 miles-per-hour in seconds. But they seldom fly more than 200 yards. Grouse do not run as fast or as far as most other upland birds. When disturbed, birds of both sexes utter a call that sounds like *pete-pete-pete.*

Many hunters call the birds partridge. But the term is a misnomer. The only true partridge in North America are the chukar and Hungarian (pages 126-127). The name ruffed grouse comes from the *ruff,* a tuft of dark feathers on the neck.

Hardwood forests with small clearings and mixed-age aspen trees make the best ruffed grouse habitat. Aspens provide good nesting cover and a year-round source of food. Grouse also favor birch trees, but will live in many other types of hardwood and conifer-hardwood forests.

Besides aspen buds, leaves and twigs, other foods include berries, fruits, clover, nuts, insects and occasionally corn. On warm, sunny days with little wind, grouse feed most of the morning and again in late afternoon. Cold, snowy or windy weather drives the birds into dense thickets or conifer stands. Grouse usually roost on the ground or in conifer trees, but when snow depth reaches 8 to 10 inches, they often burrow into the snow.

Before the spring breeding season, male grouse begin *drumming* to advertise themselves to females. A bird stands on a log, braces his body with his tail, then starts beating his wings. The sound resembles that of a one-cylinder gasoline engine starting slowly, then gradually speeding up. Some drumming continues through summer and into fall.

Grouse nest in April or May, producing a brood of eight to ten chicks. By fall, the birds are full grown and the brood scatters. Young grouse usually move at least one mile and some relocate up to 10 miles from the hatching site. Once they establish territories, they move very little the rest of their lives.

Young birds lack the wariness of those that have been pursued by hunters. Often a young grouse will sit on the ground or on a tree limb in full view of a hunter. But the birds gain experience quickly. They learn to flush well ahead, or from behind a tree or patch of dense brush where the hunter has difficulty seeing them. In remote areas, adult grouse are no more wary than young birds.

Ruffed Grouse Range

Throughout much of the North, ruffed grouse populations are cyclical, peaking about every ten years. Populations in peak years may exceed those in poor years by a ratio of 15 to 1. Biologists do not fully understand these cycles.

Signs of Grouse Activity

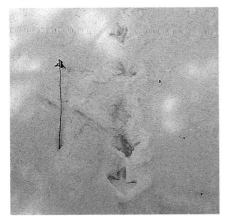

TRACKS are closely spaced and about 2 inches long. A grouse places one foot directly in front of the other, so the tracks form a straight line.

DROPPINGS on a drumming log mean that ruffed grouse are nearby. The brownish or greenish droppings are about ¼-inch in diameter.

HOLES in the snow may be burrow-roosting sites. Burrows have an entrance hole and, if the bird has left, an exit hole (above).

POINTING DOGS will pin down grouse, enabling you to get close enough for an unobstructed shot. When you move in to flush the bird, avoid walking into dense cover where shooting would be difficult.

Hunting for Ruffed Grouse

Every grouse hunter has been frustrated upon hearing a whirr of wings, scanning the dense cover, then spotting a bird just as it disappears from sight.

In early season, you may scare up a dozen grouse for every one you see in time for a shot. Even though the birds generally flush close by, leaves severely limit your range of vision. By the time the leaves fall, grouse have become spookier and tend to get up farther away. But they are much easier to see and seldom flush out of shooting range.

A good dog will improve your grouse hunting success. But a dog is not essential because grouse are easier to flush than pheasants or quail. Most hunters prefer pointing breeds, but flushers and retrievers can also be effective if they work close to the handler. Because grouse are so well camouflaged, they can be difficult to find without a good dog.

When hunting without a dog, walk through likely cover and stop frequently. You can sometimes hear the birds nervously clucking before they fly. With two or more hunters, walk on opposite sides of thick patches. One hunter is likely to get a shot when a bird flushes.

If you miss or fail to get off a shot, watch where the bird lands. A flushed bird will often fly off to a dense thicket or land in a tree. You may be able to approach close enough for a second attempt.

You can improve your success by checking the crop of a freshly-killed bird to find out what it was eating. Then, hunt where these foods are plentiful.

Grouse hunting is usually best on calm, sunny days. It seldom pays to hunt in early morning because the birds are still on their roosts. They begin moving after the woods have dried off.

A short-barreled, 20 gauge shotgun with an improved cylinder choke is an ideal grouse gun. The short barrel makes the gun easy to carry through heavy brush and enables you to swing quickly. Most grouse hunters prefer No. 7½ or 8 shot.

Grouse Hunting Techniques

WORK the edges of cover. Grouse spend much of their time feeding on fruits and berries that grow along sunlit borders. If a bird flushes, your chances of getting a clear shot are better than in a thick woods.

WALK along a logging road, powerline cut or other trail through the woods. Trails make for easy walking and the edges produce food that attracts grouse. Try to avoid backtracking along the same path.

Tips for Hunting Ruffed Grouse

PLAN your strategy using detailed maps of your hunting locale. State forestry departments may publish fire-control maps that show trails and logging roads.

ATTACH a bell to the collar of your pointing dog. This helps you keep track of its location. When the bell stops ringing, the dog is on point.

SCAN the trees as you walk. Listen for a short flutter of wings that means a grouse has hopped up to a branch. Grouse in trees evidently feel safe, often allowing hunters to approach within gun range.

LISTEN for drumming ruffed grouse while hunting. Although most drumming activity takes place in the spring, some males continue to drum into the fall, revealing their locations to hunters.

Sharp-tailed Grouse

A novice hunter may mistake a sharptail for a hen pheasant, realizing the error only after the bird sails out of range. The two are about the same size and color, but a sharptail has a short, whitish tail and usually clucks when it flushes.

Sharptails prefer large ungrazed grasslands with numerous pockets of trees and brush for cover, and fields of small grain for food. They favor wheat, oats and barley, but also eat berries, seeds, clover and buds. The birds feed in grain stubble or weed patches in early morning, loaf in wooded or brushy areas in midday, then feed again in late afternoon. Sharptails normally roost on the ground.

In early fall, a flock consists of six to eight birds. Later, many flocks combine to form a large *pack* which may have over 200 birds. When the birds flush, the flock stays together. They usually fly at least one-half mile, and occasionally a mile or more. But a bird or two may hold, so work the area thoroughly. Sharptails are strong runners and sometimes elude hunters by racing out the end of a field as the hunt begins.

Wide-ranging pointing dogs will quickly cover large fields and open brushlands where the birds are normally found. Without dogs, it is difficult to pin down a flock.

Sharp-tailed Grouse Range

Early-season hunters use 12 or 20 gauge shotguns with improved cylinder or modified chokes, and No. 6 shot. After the birds form packs, they are harder to approach, so a full choke may work better.

SHARPTAILS are named for the two long feathers in the center of the tail. The brownish back and wings are covered with white spots. Males have a patch of yellow skin above each eye. These patches are less visible after the breeding season. The birds weigh up to 2 pounds.

LOOK for sharptails in stubble fields early or late in the day. Carry binoculars to spot the birds, and listen for clucking sounds.

HUNT along brushy ravines in windy or stormy weather. A ravine, grassy ditch, or the lee side of a hill makes a good windbreak.

CHECK brush patches to find loafing sharptails. Other good loafing spots include shelterbelts and grassy areas around abandoned farms.

124

Sage Grouse

It is difficult to imagine a grouse as large as a Canada goose, but a male sage grouse may measure 30 inches long and weigh 8 pounds.

The birds inhabit open, semi-arid country with large sagebrush flats. Buds, leaves and shoots of sagebrush make up most of their diet. They also eat alfalfa, small grains, grasses, clover and berries. The birds feed along sagebrush edges in early morning. You can also find them near water holes where they eat green vegetation. They rest in gullies and draws in midday, then feed again starting in mid-afternoon.

Sage grouse flocks number only four to six birds early in the hunting season. Later, many flocks join to form packs similar to those of sharptails. The birds hold well in early season. But if hunted heavily, they soon begin to run ahead or flush wildly.

To find sage grouse, glass from a ridge in early morning. Check open areas and edges of cover. If you spot birds, attempt to stalk within gun range. If not, identify water holes, sagebrush edges and ravines that you could hunt later. A pointing dog works well in early season. But when the birds start to run, a flusher or retriever is more effective.

Sage Grouse Range

Use a 12 gauge with a modified or full choke and No. 6 shot to down sage grouse. Some hunters shoot only smaller birds. The meat of older, larger birds tends to be tough and gamey. Because a high percentage of young grouse are shot early in the season, late-season hunting tends to yield more of the older, gamey-tasting birds.

SAGE GROUSE have a mottled, grayish-brown back, a pale breast and flanks, and a black belly. The long, pointed tail feathers fan out in flight. Males have a black patch on the chin and upper neck, and a white V across the throat. Females are much smaller than males.

HUNT near stock tanks, ponds, irrigation ditches or creeks, especially in dry weather. These spots are best in early morning and just before dark. Sage grouse are seldom more than one-half mile from water.

RUSH a flock of sage grouse once you stalk within shooting range. They cannot get off the ground as quickly as other upland birds, so this tactic enables you to gain yardage for a closer shot.

Chukar Partridge

Chukars rank among the most challenging game birds. They inhabit rugged, mountainous terrain that tests the fitness of any hunter.

Named for its call, the chukar was imported from India in the late 1800s. Populations became established in arid portions of the Northwest. Typical chukar habitat varies from bare rocks to sparse grasslands. Because of the open country, the coveys are easy to see, but difficult to approach. They run uphill at the sight of a hunter. When they flush, they usually fly downhill.

Seeds, grasses, leaves and fruits make up most of the chukar's diet. The coveys, which average about 20 birds, begin feeding in mid-morning. On cool days they may feed through the afternoon. They often cover over a mile on their feeding rounds. In hot weather, chukars spend the middle of the day loafing in the shade of rocky bluffs or near springs and water holes. In windy or stormy weather, they seek depressions or crevices in the rocks.

In summer and early fall, chukars can be found at altitudes up to 11,000 feet. A heavy snowfall will drive them to much lower elevations.

Chukar Partridge Range

A 20-gauge modified-choke shotgun chambered for 3-inch shells makes a good chukar gun. It is easy to tote over steep terrain, but has a dense enough shot pattern for wild-flushing birds. Most hunters use No. 6 or 7½ shot.

CHUKARS use rocky slopes for roosting and escape cover. The birds have a grayish-brown back, a reddish bill and legs, and a black collar that passes through the eye. Black and chestnut bars cover the flanks. Chukars average about 15 inches long and weigh 18 to 24 ounces.

HUNT with pointing dogs to help pin down the birds and prevent them from running. When your dog detects fresh scent, move into shooting position quickly because chukars may not hold to a point for long.

FOLLOW chukar tracks after a fresh snowfall. In addition to providing good tracking conditions, snow makes the birds hold tighter and prevents them from running as fast as they do on bare ground.

Hungarian Partridge

In northern agricultural areas, the Hungarian partridge, or *hun,* may be the upland game bird of the future. As more heavy cover falls to the plow, populations of birds like pheasants and quail decline. But hun populations often increase.

Besides agricultural areas, huns live in rolling foothills with ample grass and sagebrush. Hunters normally find the birds in short, light cover. Huns feed mainly on grains like corn, oats, wheat and barley, but also eat weed seeds and green leaves.

Huns begin feeding after most of the dew dries off the grass. They feed until late morning, loaf in a grassy area until mid-afternoon, then resume feeding until dusk. The birds roost in alfalfa fields, grain stubble, short grass or even on plowed ground. They often form roosting rings like those of bobwhite quail. In winter, huns may roost in a depression in the snow, or burrow-roost under the snow.

Coveys normally consist of 10 to 12 birds. Huns do not hold well when first approached. They will sneak ahead of a hunter or dog, then burst from cover in unison. The covey remains together. Early in the season, huns fly only a short distance. As the season progresses, they go farther, sometimes over a half-mile.

Hungarian Partridge Range

Shotguns and shells used for huns are similar to those used for chukars. Some hunters prefer 12 gauge guns with full chokes in late season.

HUNGARIAN PARTRIDGE are technically named *gray partridge.* Native to Hungary, they have a cinnamon head and chestnut bars on the flanks. Males have a chestnut horseshoe on the breast. The birds weigh about one pound and measure 12 to 14 inches long.

WATCH the covey land, then approach the spot from opposite sides. This prevents the birds from slipping away and assures someone of a shot. You can often flush the same covey again.

HUNT with a close-working retriever or flusher, or use a pointing dog. Flushers and retrievers work best in high cover; wide-ranging pointers will find more birds in sparse grasslands or other open terrain.

Wild Turkey

A strutting gobbler with its 30-inch fan is easily the country's most spectacular game bird. Many well-traveled hunters consider the wild turkey to be the wariest game animal on the continent.

Hunters who have been outwitted by turkeys assign the birds a high level of intelligence. But the turkey's remarkable ability to elude hunters more likely results from extraordinary hearing and eyesight. They can pinpoint the source of a sound and detect even the slightest movement. When they sense anything out of the ordinary, they react instantly. A spooked turkey will run 20 miles-per-hour or burst into flight, reaching a speed of 50 to 55 miles-per-hour in seconds.

The wild turkey can adapt to a wide variety of habitats, ranging from wooded swamplands to arid grasslands. But most turkeys are found in large, mature, hardwood forests with grassy openings and plenty of oaks to supply acorns.

Turkeys spend the night in trees, flying to their roosts around sunset. They occasionally choose other elevated roosts, like powerlines. They may or may not return to the same roost on successive nights, depending on the availability of good sites.

The birds fly to the ground at first light and feed heavily until mid-morning. Occasional feeding continues through the middle of the day along with periods of resting and dusting. Feeding peaks again in mid-afternoon. Besides acorns, other favorite foods include seeds, grasses, berries, buds and insects. In northern agricultural areas, corn makes up a large part of the diet.

Turkeys often cover several miles over the course of a day. If disturbed, an entire flock may take up residence in a new location. Your chances of seeing turkeys are best on warm, clear days or in a light rain. They seldom move about or gobble during a heavy rain or when wind rustles the leaves.

In March or April, adult males, or *toms,* begin to gobble, strut, and fan their tails to interest hens. Toms choose forest clearings, trails or field edges for their breeding displays. Gobbling starts before sunrise and may continue most of the morning. Young-of-the-year males, or *jakes,* also strut, and some gobble. Toms attract a harem of up to eight hens and vigorously defend them against other males. They battle by twining their necks and attempting to spur each other. Gobbling, strutting and fighting begin to diminish once the mating season is underway.

The eggs usually hatch in June. The average brood has eight to ten chicks, or *poults.* Often two or more broods join together. A few weeks before the breeding season, the jakes leave to form their own flock. The young females stay with the hen slightly longer, usually leaving after they have bred. Adult gobblers and hens that do not breed live in separate flocks.

Hens make many sounds including putts, clucks, purrs and whines. But the voices vary widely among different birds. Toms have a gobble almost identical to that of a domestic turkey.

Wild Turkey Range

DAILY MOVEMENTS begin at dawn when turkeys leave their roosts in (1) tall trees. The birds feed in (2) areas with green vegetation and (3) harvested fields. In midday, they loaf in (4) timber with a dense canopy and dust along (5) field edges. They resume feeding in mid-afternoon and roost around sunset.

TOMS, or gobblers, can spread their tail into a large fan. They have an iridescent bronze body and a blue and red head. A fleshy red appendage, called a *dewlap*, hangs loosely from the neck and a reddish *snood* dangles just above the beak. Toms also have a *beard*, a cluster of hair-like feathers on the chest. A large tom weighs 25 pounds and has a 12-inch beard. Hens (inset) are smaller, lack iridescent coloration, and rarely have beards.

Signs of Turkey Activity

DROPPINGS of a tom (left) are usually long and J-shaped. Those of a hen (right) are shorter. But droppings of either sex may be soft with no definite shape.

DUSTING AREAS can be found along trails or roads, or in open areas with loose, dry soil and little if any vegetation. Look for tracks and signs of scratching.

Hunting for Turkey

A gobbler strutting just beyond shooting range is the supreme test of a hunter's patience. Even the blink of an eye may send the bird racing for cover.

Most states allow hunting for toms only during spring. Some also have an either-sex fall season. The best hunting method varies with the time of year.

SPRING. The most effective technique is calling like a hen to lure a gobbler within gun range. Locate gobblers at dusk by listening to their calls. Hunters refer to this technique as *putting 'em to bed*. Return the next morning and use a call that imitates the seductive sounds of a hen. Gobblers that do not have a harem often move toward the call.

FALL. Locate a flock of turkeys around a feeding or dusting area. Scatter the birds, then try to call them back. The technique works best with young birds, because they need the security of a flock and are more likely to respond to a call.

Good calling is important to turkey hunting success. The best calls differ with the conditions and the season. Learn them by listening to an experienced hunter, or to tapes or records.

Another requirement is complete camouflage. Wear drab clothing and boots, use facial makeup or a mask, and apply camouflage tape to your gun.

Shoot for the head and neck using a full-choked shotgun with No. 4 to 6 shot. Hunters who use small caliber, centerfire rifles aim for the shoulder.

ROOSTING TREES may hold from one to several dozen turkeys. Most birds select tall trees with many horizontal branches. You can identify a favorite tree by the accumulation of droppings on the ground.

How to Select and Use Turkey Calls

CALLS include friction types like (1) standard box call, (2) variation of box call, (3) peg and slate. Air-operated calls include (4) diaphragm, (5) tube, (6) bellows, (7) owl hooter.

DIAPHRAGM CALLS are hard to use but effective. They are not affected by rain and they leave your hands free. Hold the call against the roof of your mouth with your tongue.

BOX CALLS produce sounds when you scrape the chalked lid across the edge of the box. They are easy to use, but require both hands and will not work when they get wet.

130

How to Hunt Gobblers in Spring

LOCATE toms in late afternoon by using an owl hooter, or a bellows call to imitate a gobbler. If you hear a response, look for a stand 100 to 200 yards from the bird.

RETURN to your stand well before dawn. Call every 5 to 10 minutes. If you do not get an answer in a half-hour, move toward the sound of a distant tom or to another likely spot.

WAIT for a good shot. If using a shotgun, do not shoot unless the bird is within 40 yards. Fire when the head is extended. You may damage the breast meat if the head is tucked in.

Other Turkey Hunting Techniques

RUSH a flock of turkeys to scatter them into the surrounding woods. Take a stand near the spot where they flushed, then try to lure them back by making the *assembly* call of a brood hen. Where legal, some hunters use dogs to scatter turkeys and to find downed birds.

PLACE your blind near a roosting tree and start calling at dawn. Or try calling from a blind in any area where you know there are turkeys. A portable blind enables you to change location easily. This technique will work in spring and in fall.

Turkey Hunting Tips

CALL from above or from the same elevation as the turkey. The birds occasionally move downhill to a call, but the chances of them moving uphill are better.

SET OUT a decoy resembling a hen. In spring, toms may lose their normal caution and move within gun range. Be alert; other hunters may mistake your decoy for a real bird.

AVOID calling turkeys from the opposite side of an obstruction, such as a stream or fencerow. The birds are sometimes reluctant to cross a barrier when moving toward a call.

Mourning Doves

The nation's hunters harvest about 50 million doves annually, more than all other migratory game birds combined. The continent's dove population is estimated at 500 million, making it the most common game bird.

Mourning doves cannot tolerate cold weather. In northern states, the birds begin flying south after the first frost. Prior to migration, they form flocks consisting of several hundred birds.

Doves prefer open fields with scattered trees and woodlots. The birds need water each day, so there must be a pond, stock tank, flooded gravel pit or river nearby. Doves nest in grass, shrubs, stubble fields or trees, especially evergreens.

Nesting begins in early spring and continues through early fall. Doves raise up to four broods, with both parents caring for the young. After predation and weather-related losses, broods average about one bird each. This trait of raising multiple broods is unique among game birds. It assures a relatively stable population from year to year, with or without a hunting season.

Weed seeds form the bulk of the dove's diet. They favor foxtail, doveweed, ragweed and wild hemp. Other foods include corn, soybeans, sunflowers, oats and wheat.

Doves fly to their feeding areas at dawn, feed until mid-morning, then head for water. Through midday, they rest in dead or dying trees near a feeding area, a water hole or a small pond. Doves resume feeding in late afternoon, then return to a watering site late in the day.

At dusk, they fly to their roosts, often to the same trees they used during the day. If not disturbed, doves will continue to use the same roosting and watering areas.

Mourning Dove Range

Mourning doves can fly up to 55 miles-per-hour. Their normal flight is smooth, effortless and direct. But they flare quickly at the sight of hunters, darting and weaving erratically as they fly away.

Where to Find Doves

ROOSTING TREES are usually within two miles of water. A favorite roosting spot is a sand bar in a river where the birds find dead trees close to water.

WATER HOLES used by doves often have muddy water and bare ground along the edge. The best water holes have trees with dead branches nearby.

MOURNING DOVES have a slate-blue back, a fawn-colored breast with a pinkish cast, and a black spot behind the ear. They measure 11 to 13 inches from head to tail and weigh about 3½ to 5 ounces.

IDLE FIELDS attract doves because they provide an ample supply of weed seeds. Doves prefer to pick seeds from bare ground. They seldom feed in dense vegetation.

GRAVEL ROADS provide grit. Doves pick up sand and small gravel along roads in early morning and late afternoon. They also find grit along streams and in fields.

Hunting for Doves

In a dove-hunting study, observers tallied an average of eight shots for every dove bagged. The bird's elusive flight accounts for this startling statistic.

Most dove hunters simply find a stand along a commonly used flight path. It may be a route between a roosting and feeding site, or between a feeding and watering area. Conceal yourself in a brush patch or near a fenceline or tree, then pass-shoot as the birds fly through.

When selecting a stand, remember that mourning doves often fly near a dead tree, telephone pole or any object taller than the surrounding cover. They frequently fly through a gap in a treeline to reach a feeding area or water hole. Often they skirt the end of a point of cover extending into a feeding field. If stands within gun range of these spots do not produce, watch where the birds are flying and change your location accordingly.

Hunting by yourself can be difficult; the birds may land in an open field where they would be nearly impossible to approach. By stationing several hunters around the edge, you can keep the birds moving and improve shooting for everyone.

Hunting is generally best in early season. But after a few days, the birds become much warier and learn to avoid hunters. Hunting success often picks up again as migrant birds move in from the North. Most dove hunters prefer warm, calm days. The birds seldom fly in windy or rainy weather.

Dove shooters need a minimum of equipment. Camouflage clothing is ideal, but any drab outerwear will do. Many hunters use semi-automatic or pump shotguns. The repeating action enables them to keep shooting when doves are flying. A variable or screw-in choke enables you to vary your shot pattern, depending on the range of the birds. An improved cylinder or modified choke with No. 7½ or 8 shot normally works best. But in late season some hunters switch to a full choke and No. 6 shot.

LOOK for mourning doves in an area with a (1) water hole; feeding areas like (2) idle fields and (3) harvested croplands; roosting sites such as (4) trees adjacent to the water hole, (5) woodlots, (6) shelterbelts.

How to Pass-shoot for Doves

FIND a stand in the shade to reduce your visibility. But avoid any stand where overhead cover restricts your field of fire.

SELECT a spot where natural cover breaks up your outline. Even though you are not fully concealed, doves will not flare if you remain still.

USE a cooler to carry your hunting gear and to keep the birds on ice during hot weather. The cooler can also be used as a seat.

Other Dove Hunting Techniques

SET decoys on the ground or in a tree near a water hole. This will increase the chances of birds flying over your end of the pond. Hunters also place decoys in trees or on fences near feeding or roosting sites.

JUMP-SHOOT doves when they are feeding in crop fields or resting in woodlots or thickets. This technique works best during midday when the birds are not flying and pass-shooting is slow.

Woodcock

Hunters who own pointing dogs consider woodcock, or *timberdoodle,* the ideal quarry. Even with a dog inches away, a bird will hold tight, confident in its near-perfect camouflage.

Woodcock have a chunky body with a mottled brownish back and sides, and black bars on top of the head. They measure 10 to 12 inches, weigh 6 to 8 ounces, and have a bill about 2½ inches long.

Eyes on the side of the head give the birds excellent lateral vision. Some researchers believe that woodcock rely on an acute sense of hearing to find worms in the ground. The birds can fly as fast as 30 miles-per-hour. When flushed, they usually land within 100 yards.

Most woodcock breed in the northern states and Canada. They start their southerly migration in early to mid-October, leaving en masse once the ground freezes or after a heavy snow. Woodcock stop off in the same resting areas each year.

Young forests with trees 10 to 20 feet tall make the best woodcock habitat. The soil should be damp with little grassy cover. Heavy ground cover makes it difficult for the birds to find earthworms, their favorite food.

Woodcock feed mainly around dawn and dusk. Besides earthworms, the birds eat insect larvae, seeds, berries and green leaves. During the day, they rest on the ground, feeding only occasionally. In cool weather, look for them on sunny hillsides or other sunlit areas. On a hot day, they sit in the shade, often below evergreens.

The best woodcock hunting is during the migration period. Northern hunters may get some shooting at resident birds, but when the migration peaks, they may flush up to 30 birds per hour.

Hunters who use dogs flush at least twice as many birds as those who do not. Because woodcock blend in so well with the leaves, downed birds can be difficult to find without a dog.

A short-barreled 20 gauge with an improved cylinder choke is an excellent gun for woodcock. Most hunters use No. 7½ or 8 shot, but some prefer No. 9.

Woodcock Range

Tips for Hunting Woodcock

LOOK for woodcock in alder thickets. Alders generally grow in moist soil where woodcock can easily find earthworms. The birds can also be found around willows and young birch trees in damp bottomlands.

FIND a good woodcock area by looking for their dried liquid droppings, or *chalk*. The white blotches are about the size of a half dollar.

HUNT for woodcock along a moist streambank, along the edge of a swamp, or wherever you can find rich soil adjacent to water.

SHOOT while a woodcock is rising or just before it levels off. Once it begins to fly straight away, it darts and weaves, making a difficult target.

Waterfowl

When a flock of ducks or geese sets its wings and veers toward your decoys, there are few more thrilling moments in hunting.

Much of the excitement of waterfowl hunting lies in the challenge of outwitting these wary birds. A glint of light off a gun barrel or the slightest movement will cause an entire flock to flare and head for a safer landing site.

Waterfowl depend on keen eyesight to detect danger. Their wide-angle vision enables them to scan a large area quickly. They also have excellent color vision and a well-developed sense of hearing. Hunters who have stalked ducks or geese know that the slightest snap of a twig will send the flock skyward.

The birds quickly learn to avoid hunters. Within a few days after the season opens, ducks and geese know where hunters will be and seek refuge elsewhere. Sometimes thousands of birds will rest just inside the boundary of a waterfowl sanctuary.

Waterfowl are strong fliers and migrate long distances from spring breeding grounds to wintering areas. Pintails banded in Alaska have been recovered in Guatemala, nearly 5000 miles from the tagging site. Most waterfowl nest in the northern states and Canada, and winter in the southern states and Mexico. The birds follow traditional migration routes, moving at about the same time each year.

The birds use visual clues on the ground and the position of the stars to find their way. Some scientists suspect that the earth's magnetic field guides the birds' flight, especially in bad weather when they cannot see the ground or stars.

Hunters must learn in flight identification of the waterfowl common to their hunting area. All states and provinces restrict the harvest of certain species, or they may limit shooting of hens. Some states have point systems which assign values to each bird and limit your bag to a certain point total.

Identification of species and sexes requires a great deal of practice, especially with ducks. But you can recognize the major types of waterfowl by their body size and wingbeat. Geese are larger than ducks and their wingbeat is slower. *Puddle* ducks have a faster wingbeat, but not as fast as *diving* ducks.

Ducks and geese have darker meat than most upland game birds. Some people say the meat has a slight liver taste.

Waterfowl Equipment

Waterfowling requires more equipment than most other types of hunting. In the right situation, you can simply walk to a heavily-used pass, hide in the weeds and wait for the birds. But in many cases, you need decoys, camouflage clothing, waders, binoculars, calls and a duck boat.

A good blind is usually vital to successful waterfowl hunting. Where natural cover is lacking, you must construct your own blind. It may be nothing more than a length of netting or cloth. Or it may be a permanent structure complete with roof, space heater and shooting window.

Regulations may require hunters to use steel shot when hunting on state or federal waterfowl areas. The birds may pick up lead pellets from the bottom of a marsh or in a field. If they eat too many pellets, they die from lead poisoning. Steel shot is not toxic.

Steel shot has greater initial velocity than lead, but loses speed faster because it is less dense. To make up for the loss of energy, most hunters use shot a size or two larger. Number 4 steel, for example, has an effective range similar to that of No. 6 lead.

The best shotgun depends on the type of hunting you plan to do. Most hunters prefer a 12-gauge with an improved cylinder choke for close-range shooting over decoys. For pass shooting, a modified or full choke works better. Some hunters use 12 gauge magnums or even 10 gauges for long-range pass shooting, especially for geese.

FLOATING DECOYS, or *blocks*, include (1) magnum-sized cork decoy with a bell, or mushroom, weight; (2) styrofoam decoy with a lead strap for weight; (3) hollow plastic type with a scoop weight. Attach weights to the decoys with a dark-colored braided nylon cord. The length of the cord depends on water depth where you set the blocks. Decoys for field hunting include (4) wooden silhouette and (5) plastic shell.

Basic Equipment for Waterfowling

CLOTHES for waterfowl hunting include a camouflage raincoat and cap, gloves and waders. A plastic bucket stores your gear and doubles as a seat.

CALLS include (1) white-fronted goose, (2) Canada goose-wood, (3) Canada goose-plastic, (4) mallard-bellows, (5) mallard-wood, (6) mallard-plastic, (7) diving duck, (8) wood duck whistle, (9) pintail whistle. Practice your duck and goose calls by listening to a (10) tape or (11) record.

Blinds for Waterfowl Hunting

CAMOUFLAGE NETTING can be draped over trees or other natural features. This makes an inexpensive and easy-to-construct blind. The netting breaks up your outline, yet allows you to see the birds.

PIT BLINDS enable you to hunt in sparse cover, like an open field. Hunters dig pits in fields where the birds feed regularly. Some hunters line their pits with plywood and install covers to match the surroundings.

BOAT BLINDS can be moved to a new location when hunting is slow. Most are made of natural vegetation woven into chicken wire or netting.

PLATFORM BLINDS are supported by poles driven into the mud. They provide hunters with a stable base from which to shoot.

PIANO BLINDS have a shooting window that opens like a keyboard lid. They are comfortable, but birds may learn to avoid permanent blinds.

Puddle Ducks

Puddle ducks, as their name suggests, frequent shallow water. You can find them on marshes, ponds, small lakes, shallow bays of large lakes, small streams, and backwaters of large rivers. The best puddle duck waters have ample crops of submerged or floating-leaved plants for food and dense stands of emergent plants for cover.

Although most of a puddle duck's diet consists of the leaves, stems and seeds of aquatic plants, the birds may also feed on agricultural crops.

In fall, some species of puddle ducks routinely fly to cropfields in early morning where they feed on waste grain. They feed until mid-morning, then return to the water. They fly out to feed again in mid-afternoon and come back around sunset.

Large wings give puddle ducks good maneuverability. They will often circle a potential landing site several times, inspecting it closely before plopping into the water. Their leg placement gives them good balance for walking and feeding on land.

On the water, you can tell a puddle duck from a diving duck (page 148), because it rides higher with its tail well above the waterline. In the air, the wings appear larger compared to the size of its body. In hand, a puddle duck has smaller feet than a diver and legs farther forward on its body.

DABBLING, or tipping up to feed, is a puddle duck trait. They can often be seen with the front of the body submerged and the tail pointing skyward.

SPECULUMS, patches on the wing's trailing edge, are more colorful on most puddle ducks than on divers. Many puddle ducks have iridescent speculums.

VERTICAL TAKEOFF is another characteristic of puddle ducks. They spring into the air by thrusting their feet and wings downward. The large surface area of their wings gives them excellent lift. This enables the birds to take off instantly, rather than running across the water to get airborne.

MALLARDS are the most abundant duck in North America. They have a violet-blue speculum bordered by white on the leading and trailing edges. The whitish underwings stand out in flight. Hens call with a series of loud, raspy quacks. Mallards weigh about 2½ pounds.

BLACK DUCKS resemble mallards and are often called *black mallards*. But the speculum of the black duck has white only on the trailing edge. The body is brownish-black on both sexes. The hen's call is similar to that of the mallard. Black ducks average about 2½ pounds.

WOOD DUCKS can be identified in flight by their long, squared-off tails. Drakes have prominent white throat and cheek patches; both sexes have a crested head. Hens call with a loud, piercing whistle. Wood ducks weigh about 1½ pounds.

PINTAILS are named for the drake's long, pointed tail. They have a long neck and a brownish or greenish speculum. The wings are longer and narrower than those of other ducks. Drakes have a low, mellow one-note whistle. Pintails average about 2 pounds.

BLUE-WINGED TEAL have a prominent blue patch on the leading edge of the wing. Fully-plumed males have a vertical white crescent in front of the eye. Hen bluewings make a soft, high-pitched quack. Blue-winged teal average about 1 pound.

GREEN-WINGED TEAL are the smallest species of dabbler, averaging only ¾-pound. The male's chestnut head has a dark green ear patch. Hens differ from blue-wing hens by their narrower bill and white belly. Hen greenwings call with a variety of soft quacks.

WIDGEON, called *baldpate* because of the drake's white crown, have a bluish bill with a black tip and blue-gray feet. They weigh about 1¾ pounds. Drakes have a green speculum and a white patch on the leading edge of the wing, and make a three-noted whistle.

GADWALLS resemble widgeon but the inner portion of the speculum is white. They lack the white patch on the leading edge of the wing and have yellowish legs and feet. The call of a hen resembles that of a mallard, but is not as harsh. Gadwalls weigh slightly under 2 pounds.

FLOAT a winding stream to slip up on ducks. You can often surprise resting birds as you come around a bend. Hug the inside bends as long as possible so the ducks cannot see you coming. If you see a flock of ducks far ahead, get out of the boat, then sneak downstream to jump the birds.

Hunting for Puddle Ducks

A puddle duck's ability to change direction instantly makes it a difficult target. A flock of teal may suddenly appear out of nowhere, buzz your decoys, then veer off sharply and speed away before you can lift your gun.

Most hunters use 12 gauge or 20 gauge magnum shotguns for puddle ducks. The best choke depends on the hunting method.

DECOY HUNTING. Whether on water or land, successful decoy hunting depends on locating your decoy spread and blind where the birds naturally want to land. If ducks do not come to your setup, relocate in an area the birds are using.

Hunting with decoys is usually best in early morning. You should be in your blind with decoys in position before first light. Most hunters remain in their blinds until mid-morning. Hunting picks up again in mid-afternoon and stays good until sunset.

Good calling improves your chances, but poor calling is worse than none at all. Novices tend to call too often, especially when ducks are near the blind.

The most common mistake in decoy hunting is shooting too soon. Experienced hunters watch the ducks closely to read their intentions. Shoot if passing birds are in range, but do not seem interested in the decoys. Hold off if it appears they want to land. By waiting, you can shoot at birds hovering over the decoys, increasing your chances of a clean kill.

An improved cylinder choke with No. 6 or 7½ shot works best for decoy hunting, because your shots are often at close range.

JUMP-SHOOTING. Many hunters shoot over decoys in the morning, then begin jump-shooting after the birds settle into their midday resting spots.

You can jump-shoot puddle ducks by silently poling a narrow, pointed boat through tall vegetation. The shooter sits in the bow, while another hunter poles from the stern. Some hunters jump-shoot by floating winding streams.

To walk up on ducks in a small stream or pothole, approach against the wind to muffle the sound of your footsteps. On larger waters, you will have better success with the wind at your back, but you must walk quietly to prevent birds from hearing you. Ducks rest on the lee shore and would flush out of range if you approached into the wind from the opposite side.

A modified or full choke with No. 4 to 6 shot is the best all-around choice for jump-shooting.

PASS-SHOOTING. Ducks normally follow a well-defined flight path, or *pass,* as they fly between feeding and resting areas. They often funnel through a break in a treeline or a narrows between two basins of a lake. Or they routinely fly over a ridge separating two lakes. Select a likely spot, then watch the ducks carefully, because flight paths may change from day to day.

The best times to pass-shoot are usually from one-half hour before to one-half hour after sunrise, and the hour before sunset. Use a full choke with No. 2 to 6 shot, because shooting is often at long range.

How to Hunt Puddle Ducks Over Decoys

LOCATE your blind on a lee shoreline (X s), because puddle ducks prefer to land against the wind and rest in calm water. The best blinds allow you to see the birds coming from any direction.

SET your blocks within gun range and leave an open spot for the birds to land. Your spread should consist of two separate groups of decoys or one large group with an opening in the center.

CONCEAL your boat and wear camouflage clothing. Puddle ducks will check your setup closely and spot anything that looks unnatural.

CALL loudly at first. As the birds come closer, reduce the volume and call less often. Stay motionless and keep your head down.

WAIT for the best shot. The birds may circle several times, moving closer on each pass. Shoot when they cup their wings over your decoys.

Other Puddle Duck Techniques

JUMP-SHOOT by wading through flooded marsh grass or emergent vegetation along a shallow lakeshore. Walk quietly to prevent scaring up ducks out of range.

PASS-SHOOT from a strip of land between two lakes. Ducks flying from one lake to the other will choose the route that crosses the least land.

Diving Ducks

Diving ducks wing across the water in tight flocks, often only inches above the surface. They fly at amazing speeds; bluebills and canvasbacks may exceed 70 miles-per-hour.

Because it has smaller wings and legs set farther back on the body, a diving duck cannot spring into flight like a puddle duck. The smaller wings also mean less maneuverable flight. Divers usually fly straight in, rather than circling to inspect the landing site. They are not as wary as puddle ducks, but avoid approaching too close to land.

Legs in the rear of the body make it difficult for divers to walk or feed on land, but easy to swim under water. They plunge below the surface to find food and have been captured accidentally in nets set in over 100 feet of water. Diving ducks prefer to eat submerged vegetation, but they also consume animal matter like scuds, clams, snails, insects and insect larvae.

Divers lack the bright colors of many puddle ducks. Most species have contrasting black and white coloration. The speculum varies from white to dark shades of gray.

Sea ducks, also considered diving ducks, are closely related to freshwater divers. Some types of sea ducks occasionally move into inland waters, but the vast majority are taken by hunters in coastal estuaries, like Chesapeake Bay.

OPEN WATER attracts large *rafts* of divers. The birds often feed and rest in the same area. But during severe weather, they seek calmer water, frequently in protected bays.

DIVING enables the birds to feed in deep water. Because of their sleek shape and large webbed feet, diving ducks can swim long distances underwater with little effort.

TAKE-OFF requires a running start. As they race across the surface, the birds flap their wings rapidly to lift off. Once in the air, diving ducks can accelerate quickly.

SCAUP are the most common diving duck. Also called *bluebills,* they have a bluish-gray bill and a white speculum. *Greater* scaup drakes have a greenish-tinged head; *lesser* scaup purplish. Females make a soft purr. Lesser scaup average 1¾ pounds; greater scaup 2¼ pounds.

RING-NECKED DUCKS are named for the subtle chestnut ring on the drake's neck. Most hunters call them *ringbills,* because of the broad white band on the bill. In flight, they resemble scaup but lack the white speculum. Ringnecks seldom call. They weigh just over 1½ pounds.

CANVASBACKS have a long, sloping bill and forehead. The drake has a dull reddish head and makes a harsh croak; hens quack. A drake in flight shows more white than any other duck with its white back and belly. Canvasbacks weigh about 2¾ pounds.

REDHEADS in flight are often confused with mallards. Although the colors are different, the coloration pattern is the same. Drakes resemble drake canvasbacks, but have rounder heads and grayer backs. The call of a drake is a loud *meow.* Redheads weigh about 2¼ pounds.

GOLDENEYES get their name from their yellowish-gold eyes. They are also called *whistlers* because of the sound of their wingbeat. Drakes have a white cheek patch; both sexes have white breasts, bellies and speculums. Goldeneyes weigh about 2 pounds.

KING EIDERS are one of the largest ducks, averaging about 3½ pounds. The drake's body is mostly black and white, and the enlarged base of its bill stands out, even at long distances. Eiders are among 15 species of sea ducks which occur primarily along the East and West Coasts.

Hunting for Diving Ducks

Even an accomplished wingshooter has trouble leading a line of divers as they rocket past the blind. Often a hunter shoots at the first bird, but hits the second or third.

Hunting for divers is usually best in foul weather. Storms push the birds southward out of northern lakes. And bad weather will scatter rafts of divers in mid-lake, driving the birds within gun range of shore. As freeze-up approaches, most of the divers in an area become concentrated on a few deep lakes that remain open.

The guns, ammunition and hunting techniques used for diving ducks are similar to those used for puddle ducks, but with some variations.

DECOY HUNTING. Divers generally require more decoys than would be used for puddlers. Most hunters use at least three dozen and some set over 100 blocks. Because the decoys are normally set in deeper, rougher water, they must be rigged with longer cords and heavier weights.

A line of decoys extending up to 200 yards out from the blind will attract divers. The birds follow the line and swing in toward the hunters.

Some hunters look for feeding divers in open water, then set up a blind and decoys nearby. Ducks scared up in the process will soon return.

JUMP-SHOOTING. Most types of divers spend the majority of their time rafted in open water. But with a low-profile boat, you may be able to float within gun range.

Redheads and ringnecks behave much like puddle ducks, spending a good deal of time near stands of emergent vegetation. You can often pole a boat or wade to within range of the birds.

PASS-SHOOTING. Divers follow many of the same passes used by puddle ducks. Narrows, strips of land between lakes, and long points make ideal pass-shooting spots.

Diving ducks like to follow natural lines like the margin of an ice sheet or the edge of an underwater break. Watch where the birds are flying and position your blind along a heavily-used flight path.

How to Arrange Diver Decoys

SET diver decoys in a fishhook shape with the bend of the hook nearest the blind. The shank should extend into open water. Divers follow the shank and often land inside the bend. Some hunters place a few puddle duck decoys near the outside of the bend. For best results, set your decoys off a long point or island.

Tips for Decoy Hunting

ATTACH decoys at 3- to 10-foot intervals on a long cord; anchor each end. This helps you set your blocks quickly and keep them in a straight line.

PLACE confidence decoys around your blind. Gull or heron imitations may convince a flock of ducks that your set is safe.

WAVE a black flag when you spot low-flying divers. The flag may attract birds that do not see your decoys. Use a long pole for extra visibility.

Other Diving Duck Techniques

PASS-SHOOT in a narrows connecting two lake basins. Birds flying between the two basins will funnel through the constriction.

FLOAT up on ducks in open water by using a sculling boat. Let the wind blow you within range. You may be able to drift right into the raft.

Geese

The dramatic increase in the population of Canada geese is a tribute to modern wildlife management. In North America, goose numbers rose from only 750,000 in 1950 to over 2½ million three decades later. Much of this increase has resulted from the establishment of state and federal refuges throughout the nation. These sanctuaries provide a safe place for migrating birds to rest and feed.

The fall diet of geese consists mainly of waste grain, but they also eat green plants like clover, grasses and new shoots of wheat and oats. Geese feed in open fields where they can see in all directions. They seldom land next to a fenceline, a brush patch, trees, or any other cover that could spell trouble. As the flock feeds, older birds continually raise their heads to check for danger.

Flocks of geese consist of one or two family units, each numbering between four and six birds. As the migration progresses, many flocks join to form large concentrations which may number in the thousands.

An exceptional homing instinct draws geese to the same waters every year. And they often return to the same feeding areas on consecutive days. If the food supply holds up, they will come back to the exact spot in the field. Geese quickly learn to avoid fields where they have been exposed to heavy hunting pressure.

Weather has a marked effect on goose behavior. The birds spend more time feeding when the weather is cold or stormy than when it is mild. Strong winds and low clouds force geese to fly low. Under fair skies, they may fly above 10,000 feet. They do not hesitate to fly in a light rain, but they seldom move in a heavy downpour.

About three out of four geese bagged are juveniles, but some live 25 years. To survive that long, they must learn to be extremely cautious. Old birds scrutinize a landing site and veer off immediately if anything looks suspicious. Young geese are not nearly as wary.

Intelligence, which translates into wariness, seems to vary greatly among goose species. Most hunters believe that Canada geese are smartest, followed by whitefronts, and then by snows and blues.

LAKES within refuge boundaries offer sanctuary to thousands of geese. Without a safe place to rest, the birds would soon be driven away by hunters. Geese hatched on these refuges return to breed in following years.

FIELDS surrounding refuges draw feeding geese. Birds fly out within an hour or two after sunrise, feed until mid-morning, then return to water. They fly out again in mid-afternoon, then head back to the lake around sunset.

CANADA GEESE have a black head with a white chin bar. The back is grayish or brownish, and the belly is whitish. Biologists recognize 11 varieties of Canada geese, ranging in size from 4 to 12 pounds. Giant Canadas have been known to exceed 20 pounds. Large geese call with a low-pitched note followed by a much higher note.

SNOW GEESE are pure white with black wing tips. Another color phase, called *blue geese*, have a white head, but the rest of the body is slate gray. Both types call with a high-pitched yelp. They weigh 5 to 7 pounds.

WHITE-FRONTED GEESE are also called *speckle-bellies* because of the dark brown or black blotches on their chest. They have a high-pitched, laughing call. Whitefronts weigh about 6 pounds.

153

Hunting for Geese

For many hunters, the thrill of goose hunting comes from watching thousands of geese flying out to feed and listening to their piercing clamor.

Hunters accustomed to shooting ducks often have trouble hitting geese. Because the birds are so large, the tendency is to underestimate their distance and speed.

Goose hunters use 12 or 10 gauge shotguns with modified or full chokes. Shot sizes range from No. 4 to BB, although some hunters prefer buckshot.

Popular goose hunting techniques include decoy hunting, pass-shooting and stalking.

DECOY HUNTING. This technique works best in feeding fields. The key to attracting geese is to set a large number of decoys. Full-bodied decoys are bulky, so many hunters use silhouettes or shells.

Canada goose decoys will attract all types of geese. Some hunters place a few snow goose decoys off to the side, because the white color will catch the birds' attention from a greater distance. Almost any kind of white object will draw snows and blues. Hunters use popcorn bags, paper plates, wadded-up newspapers and gallon jugs. Some hunters wear white clothing or lie flat on their backs under bed sheets rather than build a blind.

PASS-SHOOTING. Most pass-shooting takes place in areas surrounding goose refuges or other waters with large concentrations of birds. Flight paths to and from a lake vary, depending on wind direction and the location of currently-used feeding fields. To select a good pass-shooting spot, spend a few hours watching the birds.

You may find better pass-shooting several miles from the refuge than near the refuge boundary. With hunters firing at them as they fly out to feed, geese learn to gain altitude quickly and are often out of range when they cross the boundary line.

STALKING. Hunters usually stalk geese after following a flock on its way out to feed. The birds almost always land in an open field where they are difficult to approach. You may have to follow several flocks to find a situation where you could make a successful stalk.

Be prepared to crawl a long distance. If you cannot get quite close enough for a shot, try rushing the birds. Geese do not spring into the air as quickly as ducks, so you can gain some yardage.

When geese land in an open field, try team-hunting. One hunter hides along an edge of the field, while another approaches from the opposite side. When the birds fly, they may pass over the hiding hunter.

How to Stalk Geese

SPOT goose flocks by driving along refuge borders or around other resting areas as feeding periods begin. Follow the birds to a field, staying far enough away so you do not disturb them. Watch where they land.

SNEAK up on the flock by using a creekbed, ditch or other depression to conceal your approach. Or crawl along a fenceline. In open terrain, low ground cover may enable you to crawl within shooting distance.

How to Hunt With Decoys in Fields

LOCATE geese in late afternoon by scouting fields surrounding resting waters. Watch until they finish feeding to make sure they are not disturbed.

PINPOINT the exact location where the flock was feeding by looking for droppings. Chances are the birds will return the next morning.

DIG a pit near the feeding site and cover the fresh dirt with vegetation. Many dig their pits at night so they are ready to hunt at daybreak.

SET decoys before dawn, but not so early that frost can accumulate. Some hunters place decoys all around their pits; others set them upwind of their pits so they can shoot birds passing overhead.

MAKE SURE geese are in range before shooting. Because of their large size, geese may be farther away than you think. As a general rule, if you can see their eyes, the birds are close enough to shoot.

Tips for Hunting Geese

PASS-SHOOT at geese flying to and from feeding areas. Many refuges allow hunting along their boundaries and some even provide blinds.

SET a large number of decoys when hunting on water; some use over 50. Leave an open spot (circle) where the birds can land.

ATTRACT geese with several callers. The sound imitates a flock of geese and is much more effective than one hunter calling by himself.

Index